FOURTH EDITION

MASS COMMUNICATION LAW IN VIRGINIA

By Cayce Myers
& W. Wat Hopkins

NEW FORUMS

NEW FORUMS PRESS INC.

Published in the United States of America
by New Forums Press, Inc.1018 S. Lewis St.
Stillwater, OK 74074
www.newforums.com

Library of Congress Cataloging-in-Publication Data Pending

This book may be ordered in bulk quantities at discount from New Forums Press, Inc., P.O. Box 876, Stillwater, OK 74076 [Federal I.D. No. 73 1123239]. Printed in the United States of America.

ISBN 10: 1-58107-295-3
ISBN 13: 978-1-58107-295-2

Table of Contents

Expanded Table of Contents

PREFACE

Mass communication law invokes images of television cameras, Web pages, celebrities, high profile trials, and landmark U.S. Supreme Court decisions. Mass communication law, however, is much more complex and nuanced. Frequently, mass communication is governed by state constitutions, statutes, and appellate court rulings, as well as decisions of lower federal courts. In short, lesser known courts and state legislatures do much of the work in creating, applying and refining mass communication law in the United States. In matters involving libel, invasion of privacy, obscenity, prior restraint and access, individual states — not the federal government — frequently have the final say. The law of mass communication, therefore, can vary considerably from state to state.

That's why this book is important. It's designed to explore those variations of the law as they exist in the Commonwealth of Virginia.

It is important to note that *Mass Communication Law in Virginia* is more encompassing than the title implies. Certainly, this book focuses primarily on law that relates to mass communication – there are chapters on libel, privacy, free press and fair trial, confidential sources, advertising and pornography. But this book goes beyond the common understanding of "mass communication law." Picketing and symbolic expression, for example, are not forms of mass communication, but they are forms of speech, as that term has been defined by the U.S.

and Virginia supreme courts. In addition, Virginia's freedom of information act is designed as a citizens' law, not a press law, though members of the press may use it more often than other citizens do. This book also includes analysis of various laws that affect technology and media platforms used by individuals and media professionals alike. So "communication law" is widely covered in this book in addition to "mass communication law."

Much has changed in mass communication legally and technolgically since the publication of the first edition of *Mass Communication Law in Virginia* in 1993. The rise of digital and social media has revolutionized mass communication. Virginia courts frequently grapple with applying older principles of communication law to new technological realities. In this edition, we discuss this new reality of mass communication in the digital age. Along with updating the laws discussed in previous editions, we have added a new chapter about the law of cyberspace and analyzed older legal principles in context with new technological realities.

Our goal in this new edition is to illustrate how mass communication laws have evolved in Virginia and affect the practice of journalism, advertising and public relations in the 21st century. Because this book focuses on both the law and its affect on mass communication, we hope it has many readers in both the legal and media industries. However, this new edition's primarily purpose is to help three specific groups: college students studying journalism or communications in the commonwealth, media professionals who need a reference book on state law as it applies to them, and high school journalists who are beginning to cope with the problems of free expression.

As with each edition, a number of people made this project easier than it could have been. Professors around Virginia who teach communication law courses sent helpful comments. This book has benefitted from the insights of both Teresa Keller of Emory and Henry College and the late Sam Riley, a colleague in the Department of Communication at Virginia Tech. Bob Hughes, formerly of Virginia Commonwealth University, and Ginger Stanley, executive director of the Virginia Press Association, made many helpful comments on the first edition.

Frosty Landon, formerly the executive director of the Virginia Coalition for Open Government, Laurence Hammack of *The Roanoke Times,* Alan Cooper formerly of *The Richmond Times-Dispatch* and Virginia Lawyers Media, provided information and comments on the second edition. Megan Rhyne, executive director of the Virginia Coalition for Open Government provided helpful information for this edition.

We are also grateful to the faculty of the Department of Communication at Virginia Tech for creating an atmosphere that makes teaching and research a pleasure.

As always, we would like to thank our wives, Roselynn Hopkins and Anne Myers, for their continuous support. Without them neither of us would be able to do very little work of any kind.

Our hope for this book is that it covers not only what the law is, but also indicates what the legal trends are in mass communication law in Virginia. There will be regular updates and, as always with law books, future editions. We hope each edition is better than the previous. We will, therefore, take each comment to heart as we continue our effort to keep track with the changes in communication law in the commonwealth. So please write or call.

Cayce Myers
Department of Communication
Virginia Tech
181 Turner Street, NW
Mail Code 0311
Blacksburg, VA 24061
(540) 231-7165
mcmyers@vt.edu

W. Wat Hopkins
Department of Communication
Virginia Tech
181 Turner Street, NW
Mail Code 0311
Blacksburg, VA 24061
(540) 231-9833
whopkins@vt.edu

For

My wife Anne and parents Tom and Linda Myers

For

Lincoln, Jonathan and Sam

1. VIRGINIA'S FREE EXPRESSION HERITAGE

Virginia is sometimes called "Mother of Presidents," because eight of the nation's chief executive officers have come from the commonwealth.[1] Virginia might also be called the "Mother of the First Amendment," however, because its contributions to free expression in the early United States are unmatched. For example:

- In 1776, Virginia became the first colony to establish legal protection for the press, a precursor to the First Amendment to the U.S. Constitution.
- Virginia's constitutional ratifying convention was the first among the states to propose that a clause ensuring press freedom be added to the Constitution.
- A Virginian, James Madison, introduced into the First Congress a document – which included two free expression provisions – that would be molded by legislative committees into the federal Bill of Rights.
- Virginia played a key role in the ratification of the Bill of Rights when, on December 15, 1791, it became the tenth state to ratify the document, ensuring that a free expression guarantee would become the law of the land.[2]

---

[1] Virginia's eight presidents are George Washington (1789-1897), Thomas Jefferson (1801-1809), James Madison (1809-1817), James Monroe (1818-1825), William Henry Harrison (1841), John Tyler (1841-1845), Zachary Taylor (1848-1850), and Woodrow Wilson (1913-1921).

[2] *See infra* note 19 and accompanying discussion.

- The Virginia Resolutions, adopted during the controversy over the Sedition Act of 1798, were instrumental in the development of the concept that citizens have the right to criticize the government and government officials. The concept would become the cornerstone for free speech protection in the United States.[3]

Virginia, therefore, has displayed a distinguished role in the heritage of free expression – a heritage that extends at least to the War for Independence, when press protection in Virginia got its first real foothold. During that war, Virginia became the first of eleven states to include a press protection clause in what was tantamount to a state constitution.[4] The document was the Virginia Declaration of Rights and grew out of a series of conventions called by Virginia colonists to deal with the increasing tension between the colonies and England. Delegates to the fifth, and final, of these conventions adopted the Resolutions for Proposing Independence on May 15, 1776. The first resolution instructed Virginia's delegates to the Continental Congress to call for a declaration of independence from England.[5]

---

[3] *See, e.g.,* New York Times Co. v. Sullivan, 376 U.S. 254, 282 (1964) (noting that the "citizen-critic" has as much a duty to criticize public officials as the public officials have to administer).

[4] Only New York and New Jersey provided no constitutional protection for the press. A good history of the press clause may be found in David A. Anderson, *The Origins of the Press Clause,* UCLA L. REV. 445, 464-73 (1983). Also helpful in the preparation of this chapter were A.E. DICK HOWARD, 1 COMMENTARIES ON THE CONSTITUTION OF VIRGINIA (1974); BERNARD SCHWARTZ, THE BILL OF RIGHTS (1971).

[5] North Carolina's delegates to the Continental Congress received the same instructions more than a month before

The second resolution provided for the establishment of a committee to prepare a declaration of rights and "a plan of government" to maintain order and secure liberty for Virginia residents.[6] Twenty-eight members were appointed to the committee, but, ironically, two men who would become key members were not among the original twenty-eight. James Madison, who would draft the document that would be molded into the federal Bill of Rights, was added to the committee May 16, and George Mason, who would ultimately draft the Declaration of Rights, was added May 18.

Within a month of his appointment, Mason had finished the Declaration of Rights. It was adopted June 12, 1776, and contained this provision: "That the freedom of the press is one of the greatest bulwarks of liberty, and can never be restrained but by despotic Governments."[7]

Constitutional historian Bernard Schwartz called the document "the first true Bill of Rights in the modern American sense."[8] The 1776 Virginia Convention was important for another reason. As Schwartz wrote, it was:

> [C]rucial in the history of the federal Bill of Rights, both as the first constitutional instrument upon which the Federal Bill of Rights was modeled and as the training-ground

---

Virginia's – on April 12, 1776 – making North Carolina the first of the colonies to advocate freedom from England.

[6] *See* SCHWARTZ, *supra* note 4, at 231.

[7] *Id.* at 235, 243. North Carolina's press clause was modeled on this provision. *See id.* at 287. *See also* Anderson, *supra* note 4, at 538.

[8] *Id.* at 231.

of the man who was later to become known as the father of both the federal Constitution and its Bill of Rights.[9]

The father of the Bill of Rights, however, did not always favor the attachment of such a bill to the Constitution. James Madison was originally among those federalists who believed a bill of rights to be unnecessary since the Constitution did not give the federal government the power to usurp the rights ostensibly protected in such a bill.

Other Virginians disagreed. George Mason, for example, attempted without success to have the Constitutional Convention create a committee to draft a bill of rights in that hot, Philadelphia summer of 1787.[10] And during the state ratifying conventions on the Constitution, Virginia was the first of three states to propose the attachment of a federal press clause, doing so June 17, 1788.[11] Virginia's proposal, which included protection for speech as well as the press, read: "That the people have a right to freedom of speech, and of writing and publishing their sentiments, that the freedom of the press is one of the greatest bulwarks of liberty and ought not to be violated."[12]

The support in Virginia for the inclusion of a bill of rights to the federal Constitution made an impact on Madison. Indeed, one fellow Virginian who

---

[9] *Id.*

[10] *Id.* at 438. The failure of the convention to adopt a bill of rights may be among the reasons that Mason did not sign the completed Constitution.

[11] *See* Anderson, *supra* note 4, at 471. New York and North Carolina were the other two.

[12] Va. Ratifying Convention (1788), *in* 2 SCHWARTZ, *supra* note 4, at 762, 842.

voiced strong support for a bill of rights was James Monroe, Madison's opponent for a seat in the First Congress. Monroe made Madison's failure to call for a bill of rights a key issue in the campaign.[13] And, while Madison eventually became committed to the inclusion of a bill of rights, his first support for the bill was because he recognized that its absence made adoption of the Constitution tenuous.[14]

Madison, therefore, struck a bargain with opponents of the Constitution: He agreed to introduce into Congress a proposed bill of rights in exchange for support for the Constitution in Virginia.[15] The bargain worked. Madison was elected to the House of Representatives; the Constitution was ratified; and, on June 18, 1788, one month after Congress opened, Madison introduced into the House his proposed bill of rights. The bill contained two amendments protecting expression:[16]

> The people shall not be deprived or abridged of their right to speak, to write, or to publish their sentiments; and the freedom of the press, as one of the great bulwarks of liberty, shall be inviolable.
>
> . . . .
>
> No state shall violate the equal rights of conscience, or the freedom of the press, or the trial by jury in criminal cases.

---

[13] *See* Anderson, *supra* note 4, at 476

[14] *Id.* at 476-77.

[15] *See* LEONARD LEVY, EMERGENCE OF A FREE PRESS 254-55 (1985).

[16] The various versions of the speech and press clauses quoted here are published in Anderson, *supra* note 4, at 538-41.

The second provision was included, apparently, because Madison did not believe the Bill of Rights, as part of a federal document, would automatically apply to state action.

Madison's bill was referred to a select committee, which drafted this language protecting speech and the press:

> The freedom of speech and of the press, and the right of the people peaceably to assemble and consult for their common good, and to apply to the Government for a redress of grievances, shall not be infringed.

After debates in the House, the Bill of Rights was adopted and sent to the Senate. The Senate also adopted the bill, again altering the language of the speech and press clauses:

> That Congress shall make no law, abridging the freedom of speech, or of the press, or the right of the people peaceably to assemble and consult for their common good, and to petition the government for a redress of grievances.

It is unclear why the Senate inserted the specific reference to Congress. It may have been a simple editorial change, or it may have been a concerted effort to restrict Congress and only Congress. At any rate, a conference committee made up of House members and senators eventually hammered out a final Bill of Rights. On September 25, 1789, the speaker of the house and the vice president signed a resolution asking President George Washington to send the 12 amendments to the governors of the states for ratification. The first two amendments were not adopted and what had been the third amendment became the first:[17]

> Congress shall make no law respecting an establishment of religion, or prohibiting the free exercise thereof; or abridging the freedom of speech or of the press, or the right of the people peaceably to assemble, and to petition the Government for a redress of grievances.[18]

Amendments to the Constitution require ratification by three-fourths of the states.[19] That occurred December 15, 1791, when Virginia became the tenth of 13 states to ratify the Bill of Rights.

Madison's proposed amendment restricting state interference with freedom of expression, of course, was not part of the bill. Virginia adopted much of the language from that proposed amendment in its state constitution, however, where it remains today:

> That the freedom of speech and of the press are among the great bulwarks of liberty, and can never be restrained except by despotic governments; that any citizen may freely speak, write, and publish his sentiments on all subjects, being responsible for the abuse of that right; that the General Assembly shall not pass any law abridging the freedom of speech or of

---

[17] The first amendment in the original Bill of Rights related to the apportionment of members of the House of Representatives, and the second amendment related to changing compensation for members of Congress.

[18] U.S. CONST. amend 1.

[19] U.S. CONST. art. V.

the press, nor the right of the people peaceably to assemble, and to petition the government for a redress of grievances.[20]

The free expression clauses of neither the Bill of Rights nor the Virginia Constitution have eliminated efforts to control speech and press, however. Within seven years of the adoption of the Bill of Rights, which specifically provided that Congress make no law abridging those freedoms, Congress passed a law doing just that.

The Sedition Act was one of a series of laws passed during the anxious early days of the republic when the Federalists and Republicans were debating the type of government that would work best under the Constitution – a strong democracy guided by the will of the people or a conservative government with relatively strict controls.

The Sedition Act, which made it a crime to criticize the Congress or the president, was designed to silence the vituperative anti-Federalist press.[21]

Virginia responded with a series of resolutions calling for the repeal of the act. Madison, who drafted the resolutions, argued that the federal government did

---

[20] VA. CONST. art 1, § 12. For a summary of the changes in the provision over the years, *see* 1 HOWARD, *supra* note 4, at 251-54.

[21] The Sedition Act provided than any person who "shall write, print, utter, or publish. . . any false, scandalous or malicious writing. . . against the Government of the United States, or either house of the Congress. . . or the President. . . or to excite against them the hatred of the good people of the United States. . . or to resist or oppose, or defeat any such law. . . shall be punished by a fine not exceeding two thousand dollars, and by imprisonment not exceeding two years." U.S. Statutes at Large 1, § 2 (1798), at 596.

not have the power to pass the restrictions and that they contradicted a free society. The Sedition Act, he wrote, "[I]s levelled against the right of freely examining public characters and measures and of free communication among the people thereon, which has ever been justly deemed the only effectual guardian of every other right."[22]

The Virginia Resolutions of 1798 helped establish the theory that a key purpose of the First Amendment was to provide citizens the freedom and protection to criticize their government and their governors. That theory has become a bedrock of free expression in the United States.[23]

Virginia, therefore, has possibly the strongest free expression heritage among the thirteen original states. Whether modern Virginia law remains true to that heritage, however, is not so clear. Indeed, the Virginia Supreme Court has demonstrated a singular lack of understanding of First Amendment principles, as demonstrated by the number of free speech cases from Virginia that the U.S. Supreme Court has overturned. Those cases cover many areas of free speech jurisprudence: prior restraint,[24] post-publication punishments,[25] access to courtrooms,[26]

---

[22] James Madison, *Report of the Committee to Whom Were Referred the Communications of Various States, Relative to the Resolutions of the Last General Assembly of this State, Concerning the Alien and Sedition Laws, in* THE MIND OF THE FOUNDER: JAMES MADISON 243 (M. Myers ed., 1981).

[23] *See, e.g.,* New York Times Co. v. Sullivan, 376 U.S. 254, 282 (1964).

[24] Bigelow v. Virginia, 421 U.S. 809 (1975).

[25] Landmark Commc'ns v. Virginia, 435 U.S. 829 (1978).

[26] Richmond Newspapers v. Virginia, 448 U.S. 555 (1980).

forced oaths,[27] obscenity prosecutions,[28] defamation,[29] civil rights activities,[30] and expressive conduct.[31]

Despite the First Amendment, therefore, and the Constitution of Virginia, which arguably offers more free speech protection than the federal document, persons who exercise their free speech rights in Virginia are often in jeopardy.

---

[27] Skull v. Virginia, 359 U.S. 344 (1959).

[28] Lee Art Theatre v. Virginia, 392 U.S. 636 (1968).

[29] Letter Carriers, AFL-CIO v. Austin, 418 U.S. 264 (1974).

[30] NAACP v. Button, 371 U.S. 415 (1963).

[31] Virginia v. Black, 538 U.S. 343 (2003).

2. VIRGINIA'S COURTS

The best way to win a lawsuit, lawyers sometimes say, is to keep it out of court. Courtrooms are unpredictable places, and one can never be sure what action a judge may take or what decision a jury may deliver.

In a judicial system, however, "Uniformity of practice is regarded as a vital element,"[1] so courtrooms also possess a certain predictable nature. Protocol must be followed; there is strict adherence to procedure; rules of evidence are not violated; and, in the end, legal disputes are settled.

Those disputes are settled in Virginia much as they are in any other state: Two types of cases – criminal and civil – are adjudicated in one of two types of court – federal and state; juries determine the facts of a case while judges and justices determine whether the law is properly applied.[2] The system is not perfect, but it works well, and, as judges are wont to say, there is no constitutional guarantee to a perfect trial – only to a fair trial.

---

[1] VIRGINIA COURTS IN BRIEF, http://www.courts.state.va.us/courts (last visited Oct. 20, 2015). The Web page of the Virginia judicial system, from which this document is available in PDF form, is a robust source of information about courts in Virginia, including the state supreme court and court of appeals. It also has links to the Web pages of all circuit courts that have such pages.

[2] A good discussion of court systems can be found *in* Thomas A. Schwartz & Cayce Myers, *The Law in Modern Society, in* COMMUNICATION AND THE LAW 1 (W. Wat Hopkins ed., 2016).

COURTS IN GENERAL

The mission of Virginia's court system is "to assure that disputes are resolved justly, promptly, and economically."[3] Those disputes may be between the government and an individual or between individuals.

If the government is party to a lawsuit, the suit is generally, though not always, a criminal case. A representative of the state – called the "district attorney" or "prosecuting attorney" in some states and called the "commonwealth's attorney" in Virginia – brings an action and, if the individual – called a "defendant" – is found guilty, the result may be a fine paid to the government, a jail or prison sentence, or both.

In civil actions, on the other hand, the state is not a party, but acts as a referee, providing the framework by which a judge and jury determine the issues in the case. A civil action is brought by one person against another when a dispute cannot be settled otherwise. Corporations and other legal entities may also be parties in lawsuits. The prevailing party in a civil action wins monetary damages, or the court may order some action to be taken, but no prison sentence is involved.

In both criminal and civil actions juries are called upon to determine the facts. The jury is the sole determiner of the facts. That is, once the jury determines that certain actions occurred, that determination can be changed only in rare circumstances. On appeal, a court may determine that there were errors in the application of the law, and those errors may be of such magnitude that the jury's determination of the facts was prejudiced. If that is the

---

[3] VIRGINIA COURTS IN BRIEF, *supra* note 1.

case, the appellate court can order a new trial and can order that the new trial be held in accordance with its findings, but the appellate court cannot change the jury's determination of the facts in the case.

Lawsuits are adjudicated in either state or federal courts, depending upon jurisdiction.[4] If both parties in a civil dispute are residents of Virginia or if there is a violation of state law or local ordinances, the dispute is settled in a state court. If one party is a resident of Virginia and the second party is a resident of some other state, however, or if there is a violation of federal law, the dispute is settled in a federal court. In addition, lawsuits claiming violation of some constitutional right are adjudicated in federal courts.

Commonwealth of Virginia Courts

Three types of trial courts exist in Virginia: circuit courts, juvenile and domestic courts and general district courts.[5]

Circuit courts are the highest trial courts in the commonwealth. One-hundred twenty-two courts operate in 31 circuits. Circuit courts have exclusive, original jurisdiction in criminal felony cases and in all civil cases in which claims are for more than $25,000.[6] They also have appellate jurisdiction over matters

---

[4] "Jurisdiction" refers to the authority of the court or the domain over which a court holds authority. Virginia courts, for example, hold jurisdiction over persons who reside in Virginia or who are subject to Virginia law.

[5] Virginia Courts in Brief, *supra* note 1, and other resources on the Web page of the Virginia judicial system, *supra* note 1, were helpful in the preparation of this chapter.

[6] A felony is any crime punishable by commitment to a state penitentiary (rather than a local jail). Crimes that are not felonies are called "misdemeanors." They are punishable by no more than one year in jail, fines up to $1,000 or both.

heard in district courts. Judges are appointed by the General Assembly for eight-year terms.

District court judges are appointed for six-year terms in each of Virginia's 32 judicial districts. District courts have jurisdiction in all matters where claims do not exceed $4,500 and in some matters where claims are more than $4,500 but less than $25,000.[7] District courts also have jurisdiction in misdemeanor criminal offenses and in violations of local ordinances. In addition, special district courts have jurisdiction over matters involving juveniles and families.[8]

Appeals in Virginia are heard by the Virginia Court of Appeals and the Virginia Supreme Court. Only in rare cases – when the death penalty is imposed, for example – is appeal to either of these courts automatic or by right. In most cases, a petition for appeal must be made, and the court can accept or refuse the case.

Appeals in criminal, traffic and domestic cases are made to the Virginia Court of Appeals, as are appeals from decisions of administrative agencies. The decision of the court of appeals in all but criminal matters is final; decisions in criminal cases may be appealed to the Virginia Supreme Court. Appeal in most civil matters is directly to the state supreme court.

Judges to the court of appeals are appointed by the General Assembly for eight-year terms; the chief judge is selected from among the 11 judges on the court. Supreme court justices are appointed for 12-

---

[7] A separate small claims division of the district court has jurisdiction over civil matters when the claim does not exceed $5,000.

[8] A juvenile in Virginia is any person aged 17 or younger.

year terms; the chief justice is selected from among the seven justices on the court.

The justices of the state supreme court and the judges of the court of appeals are listed in Chart 1.

Chart 1. VIRGINIA APPELLATE COURTS

Court of Appeals	Supreme Court
Glen A. Huff, Chief Judge Rossie D. Alston Jr. Richard Y. Atlee Jr. Randolph A. Beales Teresa M. Chafin Marla Graff Decker Robert J. Humphreys Stephen R. McCullough Mary Grace O'Brien William G. Petty Wesley G. Russell Jr.	Donald W. Lemons, Chief Justice S. Bernard Goodwyn D. Arthur Kelsey William C. Mims Elizabeth A. McClanahan Cleo E. Powell Jane Marum Roush

FEDERAL COURTS IN VIRGINIA

Virginia is divided into two federal districts, each with its own trial court.[9]

The U.S. District Court for the Eastern District of Virginia has 17 judges who hold court in Richmond, Norfolk and Alexandria.[10] The U.S. District Court for the Western District has four judges who hold court in Abingdon, Big Stone Gap, Charlottesville, Danville,

---

[9] The Web site for the U.S. District Court for the Eastern District of Virginia is http://www.vaed.uscourts.gov; the Web site for the U.S. District Court for the Western District of Virginia is http://www.vawd.uscourts.gov.

[10] Though the judges hold court in Norfolk, their chambers – or offices – are located only in Alexandria and Richmond. *See* Chart 2.

Harrisonburg, Lynchburg and Roanoke.[11] The federal district court judges and their courts are displayed in Chart 2.[12]

Chart 2. U.S. District Courts

Eastern District of Virginia	Western District of Virginia
Alexandria Leonie M. Brinkema Gerald Bruce Lee Liam O'Grandy Anthony J. Trenga *Norfolk* Rebecca Beach Smith, Chief Judge Raymond A. Jackson Mark S. Davis Arenda Wright Allen *Richmond* Henry E. Hudson John A. Gibney Jr. M. Hannah Lauk	*Abingdon* James P. Jones *Roanoke* Glen E. Conrad, Chief Judge Elizabeth K. Dillon Michael F. Urbanski

[11] Though there are federal courthouses in all the listed cities, judges' chambers – or offices – are located only in Abingdon and Roanoke. *See* Chart 2.

[12] In addition to federal judges, both district courts have senior judges and magistrate judges. Senior status is form of semi-retirement. Judges maintain offices and reduced case loads. Magistrate judges are appointed by the district court and generally oversee first appearances of criminal defendants, set bail, and conduct other administrative duties.

Chart 3. Federal Courts of Appeals

Judges of the Fourth U.S. Circuit Court of Appeals	**U.S. Courts of Appeal & District Courts Over Which They Hold Jurisdiction**[13]
William B. Traxler, Chief Judge G. Steven Agee Albert Diaz Allyson K. Duncan Henry F. Floyd Roger L. Gregory Pamela A. Harris Barbara Milano Keenan Robert B. King Diana Gribbon Motz Paul V. Niemeyer Dennis W. Shedd Stephanie D. Thacker J. Harvie Wilkinson III James A. Wynn Jr. Clyde H. Hamilton (Senior Judge) Andre M. Davis (Senior Judge)	*1st Circuit*: Maine, Massachusetts, New Hampshire, Rhode Island, Puerto Rico
	2d Circuit: Connecticut, New York (4), Vermont
	3d Circuit: Delaware, New Jersey, Pennsylvania (3), the Virgin Islands
	5th Circuit: Louisiana (3), Mississippi (2), Texas (4)
	6th Circuit: Kentucky (2), Michigan (2), Ohio (2), Tennessee (3)
	7th Circuit: Illinois (3), Indiana (2), Wisconsin (2)
	8th Circuit: Arkansas (2), Iowa (3), Minnesota, Missouri (2), Nebraska, North Dakota, South Dakota
	9th Circuit: Alaska, Arizona, California (4), Guam, Hawaii, Idaho, Montana, Nevada, Northern Mariana Islands, Oregon, Washington (2)
	10th Circuit: Colorado, Kansas, New Mexico, Oklahoma (3), Utah, Wyoming
	11th Circuit: Alabama (3), Florida (3), Georgia (3)
	D.C. Circuit: District of Columbia
	Federal Circuit: National jurisdiction in administrative law, intellectual property and certain other claims.

[13] The numbers in parentheses indicate the number of federal district courts in the state, if more than one.

In addition, the Fourth U.S. Circuit Court of Appeals is located in Richmond. Appeals from the two district courts in Virginia – as well as from federal district courts in Maryland, North Carolina, South Carolina and West Virginia – go to the Fourth Circuit. The judges of the Fourth Circuit appear in Chart 3, as does a listing of the other 12 federal circuit courts and the states from which federal courts are appealed to those courts.

A Sample Case

A good way to demonstrate how the court system works is to follow a typical case from the birth of a dispute through disposition.[14]

In this case, Mayor Ira Crotchity of Boondocks is suing the *Boondocks Daily Bungler* for libel[15] Crotchity complains that the *Bungler* defamed him when it published an article reporting that he violated state conflict of interest laws by awarding the town's tire contract to his own Crotchity Tire Co. The tire company was once owned by the mayor, but, unbeknownst to the newspaper, the mayor has divested himself of any interest in the company. Crotchity is seeking $100,000 for his damaged reputation.

The case is called *Crotchity v. Boondocks News Co.* The name of the party bringing the action is always first in the title of a case. In addition, legal names of individuals and companies must be used.

---

[14] A more complete case study is *in* MARC FRANKLIN, THE BIOGRAPHY OF A LEGAL DISPUTE (1984).

[15] The names Mayor Ira Crotchity, Boondocks, *Boondocks Daily Bungler*, Boondocks News Co. and Crotchity Tire Co., and the facts of this sample case are entirely fictional and are not intended to represent any person, town, newspaper, company or libel suit.

The name of the newspaper may be the *Boondocks Daily Bungler,* but the newspaper is owned by a company, and it is the company that is being sued. The party bringing the suit is the *plaintiff*; the party being sued is the *defendant*. If the case is a criminal action begin brought against an individual – for illegally burning a cross, for example – the jurisdiction bringing the charges would be the plaintiff, and the person charged with the crime would be the defendant, as in *Commonwealth v. Black.*[16]

Crotchity's attorneys must see to it that the Boondocks News Co. is properly notified of the lawsuit. To do so, they must ensure that a copy of the lawsuit is served on a representative of the company. In a state case, this is generally done by a deputy sheriff. A copy of the suit is also filed in the clerk of court's office for the circuit court that holds jurisdiction. The lawsuit must specify the actions the News Co. took that Crotchity believes to be improper, and it must describe how those actions harmed him. The case is filed in a circuit court because Crotchity is seeking more than $25,000 in damages.

Once the News Co. is served, it has 28 days in which to file a response. If a defendant does not respond to a lawsuit, an order will be entered finding in favor of the plaintiff. In this case, the newspaper is likely to file a *demurrur* – a statement acknowledging that the article was published, but arguing that publication of the article was not improper.

---

[16] The cross-burning case that eventually became *Virginia v. Black* is discussed in Chapter 3. While that case began as *Commonwealth v. Black*, when it was accepted by the Supreme Court of the United States, "Commonwealth" was replaced by "Virginia" in its name.

After the newspaper files its answer, the legal maneuvering will begin. Pleadings – legal arguments – will be filed; depositions will be taken; motions will be filed and argued. Depositions are statements from potential witnesses that are taken in the form of testimony outside the courtroom. Television courtroom dramas notwithstanding, very few surprises occur in courtrooms, and there are virtually no surprise witnesses. Attorneys for both sides know what most witnesses are going to say in court long before those witnesses take the stand.

If the case is not settled before its trial date, a jury will be empaneled. Evidence will be taken, first from the plaintiff, then from the defendant. The plaintiff's evidence is designed to meet what is called a "burden of proof." The burden of proof consists of certain elements – in a libel action, there are generally six (discussed in Chapter 5).

The Boondocks News Co. can win the libel action by either demonstrating that Crotchity has not proved all the elements of his burden of proof or by offering a justification – an affirmative defense – for publishing the alleged defamation.

After both the plaintiff and defendant have finished presenting evidence, the judge explains the law in the case and instructs the jury as to the options it has in deciding upon a verdict. Attorneys for both sides then argue their cases to the jury. That is, the attorney for each sides interprets the evidence for the jury in a light that best supports the position of that attorney's client. The jury then deliberates with a goal of reaching a verdict.

Regardless of who wins, the case is likely to be appealed. If the News Co. wins and Mayor Crotchity appeals, the name of the case will remain the same. If

Mayor Crotchity wins and the News Co. appeals, however, the name of the case will change to *Boondocks News Co. v. Crotchity,* because the company, not Crotchity, is now bringing the action.

A party cannot appeal a case simply because the party does not like the verdict. The argument that a jury decided a case wrongly is not grounds for appeal. The appeal must be based on allegations that the judge in some way misapplied the law – that is, that the judge allowed evidence to be heard that should not have been heard or did not allow evidence that should have been heard. The application of the law, not the facts decided by the jury, is what is appealable.

As previously indicated, the appeal of a civil action is to the Virginia Supreme Court, and the court may or may not accept the appeal. If the court refuses, for all practical purposes, the case is over – a case cannot leap-frog the state's highest court to the U.S. Supreme Court.

If the court accepts the case, all documents from the trial and a transcript of the trial are sent to the court. In addition, attorneys for Crotchity and the newspaper company will file legal briefs – written arguments describing the major points the attorneys will argue to the court and cases the attorneys say support those arguments. The court will hear oral arguments from both sides and will render an opinion.

Once again, the case will likely be appealed by the party against whom the state supreme court rules. The appeal is to the U.S. Supreme Court by what is called a *writ of certiorari.* And again, the Supreme Court may not accept the case. If the court denies *cert,* the appeal of opinion of the state supreme court stands as the final disposition. If the Supreme Court grants *cert,* the appeal process is repeated and the Supreme Court will determine the final outcome of the case.

The procedure for a libel action filed in a federal court is similar. A case would go to federal district court if there is what is called a "diversity of citizenship." If the alleged defamation about which Crotchity complained was published by a media organization in another state, for example, there would be a diversity of citizenship, and Crotchity would have filed his suit in a federal district court rather than a state circuit court. In such a case, a federal court is required to apply the law of Virginia – the state in which the federal court where the suit was filed. Appeals to federal district courts in Virginia go to the Fourth U.S. Circuit Court of Appeals in Richmond and, from there, are appealed to the U.S. Supreme Court.

3. RESTRAINTS ON EXPRESSION

Communication law is often complicated and controversial. While free expression is guaranteed by the First Amendment of the U.S. Constitution and every state constitution, the parameters of that freedom remain in dispute: What types of speech deserve protection? When is material obscene? Should broadcasters be required by law to provide certain types of public interest programming? Is libel law in need of reform for the sake of equity? When does the right of free expression outweigh other constitutionally protected rights?

Upon one point virtually all disputants agree, however: At a minimum, the free expression guarantees were designed to ensure that the government not be allowed to censor the press or the speech of individuals. Even so, courts, lawmakers and individuals often disagree on how far the prohibition against prior restraint should be taken.

The U.S. Supreme Court, for example, has said that fighting words, defamation, obscenity and speech that causes a threat to national security may be restrained.[1] The Supreme Court of Virginia has similarly noted that the guarantees of free speech and press in the First Amendment and in the Virginia Constitution are not absolute.[2]

---

[1] *See, e.g.,* Roth v. U.S., 354 U.S. 476 (1957); Chaplinsky v. New Hampshire, 315 U.S. 568 (1942); Near v. Minnesota, 283 U.S. 697 (1931).

[2] *See* Landmark Commc'ns v. Commonwealth, 233 S.E.2d 120, 124 (Va. 1977), *rev'd* 435 U.S. 829 (1978). At the

The question generally addressed by the courts, therefore, is not *whether* lines should be drawn prohibiting the publication of certain material, but *where* those lines should be drawn. This chapter focuses on efforts by Virginia courts to draw those lines.

Efforts to restrain speech in Virginia are not unusual. This despite the claim by the Virginia Supreme Court that the commonwealth's constitutional protection of speech and press is more encompassing than that granted by the federal constitution.[3] Efforts to censor speech in the commonwealth, however, have generally been accompanied by bitter debate.

In April 1993, for example, the Fairfax County library board, in the face of legal threats, voted 9-3 to keep the *Washington Blade* in its collections and in the lobbies of the system's twenty-two branch libraries. The weekly, gay-oriented newspaper had been in the library system's periodical collections since 1985, but some patrons complained in December 1992 when library officials allowed the paper to be distributed in the lobbies of branch libraries. Opponents of the newspaper threatened to sue the county for promoting sodomy, which was then illegal in Virginia,[4] but the

---

U.S. Supreme Court level the case is titled *Landmark Communications v. Virginia*.

[3] Robert v. Norfolk, 49 S.E.2d 697, 700 (Va.1948). *See* quotation accompanying *infra* note 77. Prior restraint is defined in this chapter as any effort by the government to restrain expression, including post-expression punishment. The Virginia Supreme Court, however, does not consider post-expression punishment as a form of prior restraint. *See infra* note 28.

[4] *See Virginia Library to Keep Gay Paper,* EDITOR & PUBLISHER, May 8, 1993, at 11.

lawsuits didn't materialize. The Montgomery-Floyd Regional Library came under similar attack when residents complained that it held in its collections *Daddy's Roommate,* a children's book about the daily life of a gay father and his partner.[5]

Almost as heated was a dispute over the Confederate flag in Danville in March 1995. The Danville City Council ordered the flag removed from the city's Museum of Fine Arts and History in September 1993. The Danville Chapter of the Heritage Preservation Association, however, raised sufficient funds to erect a Civil War monument at the museum site and convinced the city council – over the votes of the council's two black members – that the Confederate flag should be flown atop the seven-foot-tall granite obelisk.[6]

A similar dispute erupted in Lexington in 2011 when the city council passed an ordinance that allowed only three flags to fly on city owned flag standards affixed to light poles: the U.S. flag, the state flag of Virginia, and the city flag of Lexington. The ordinance was passed in light of public outcry over the Sons of Confederate Veterans flying the Confederate flag on various city flag standards attached to light poles during a Lee-Jackson parade earlier in the year. The SCV sued Lexington alleging that the city violated the SCV's First Amendment rights as well as a 1991 consent decree that banned Lexington from "denying

---

[5] *See* Mara Lee, *Library Board Delays Decision on Book,* ROANOKE TIMES, Mar. 17, 1994, at C1.

[6] *See* Wes Allison, *Confederate Flag Waves in Danville,* RICHMOND TIMES-DISPATCH, Mar. 27, 1995, at A1; Wes Allison, *Following the Flag Into Battle,* RICHMOND TIMES-DISPATCH, Mar. 28, 1995, at B1.

or abridging the rights of the SCV and its' members."[7] Ultimately the U.S. Court of Appeals for the Fourth Circuit held that Lexington's ordinance was constitutional. The court held that even though the flag standards were a designated public forum the city's ordinance was not designed to "exclude either a specific speaker or a specific class of speech."[8]

The issue of Confederate symbols has been an issue in private spheres as well. In 2013 the Virginia Flaggers, a pro-Confederate flag group, faced public backlash when they attempted to publically display a Confederate flag along Interstate 95 in Chesterfield County near Richmond. The display of the Confederate flag was a reaction to state and municipal governments' removal of the flag at historic sites.[9] Although several politicians and the NAACP opposed the use of Confederate flags flown conspicuously on private property, the flag remains a point of controversy in the Richmond community.[10]

---

[7] Sons of Confederate Veterans v. City of Lexington, 722 F.3d 224, 227 (4th Cir. 2013). The consent decree issued in 1993 involved the City of Lexington banning the SCV from displaying a Confederate flag during a parade honoring the re-dedication of a statue of Stonewall Jackson in 1991. *See* Sons of Confederate Veterans, Va. Div. v. City of Lexington, No. 7:93-CV-00492 (W.D. Va. 1993).

[8] *Id.* at *5.

[9] *See* Cameron McWhirter, *New Front in Running Battle Over Rebel Flag*, WALL STREET J., Sept, 6, 2013, at A4.

[10] *See* Susan Svrluga, *A Confederate Flag Divides a Virginia Community*, WASH. POST, Aug. 1, 2015, *available at* https://www.washingtonpost.com/local/a-confederate-flag-divides-a-virginia-community/2014/08/01/118792ae-18e6-11e4-9349-84d4a85be981_story.html.

Debate over expression also involves advertising. In 1996, threats forced an advertising company to remove a billboard that simply proclaimed "Diversity Enriches." No one had complained about the billboard on a heavily traveled road in Christiansburg until a photo appeared in a newspaper. Then, Frank Amburn of Outdoor East Advertising said he received more than fifty calls, most complaining about the sponsors of the billboard: "Gay & Straight Citizens of Southwest Va." Some callers threatened to destroy other billboards placed by the company, so Amburn decided to replace the message and issue a refund.[11] Conversely, in 2014, Parents and Friends of Ex-Gays and Gays, known as PFOX, posted a billboard along Interstate 95 near downtown Richmond titled "No one is born gay" to express their view that homosexuality was a choice. The billboard was widely criticized by LBGT rights organizations who were outraged at what they argued was an anti-gay message.[12] In response to the billboard's message, the Gay Community Center of Richmond planned a group photo of more than 400 people who support LBGT rights.[13]

---

[11] *See* Kathy Loan, *Ad Manager: Threats Killed "Diversity" Billboard,* ROANOKE TIMES, Jan. 25, 1996, at C1.

[12] *See* Nicole Hensley, *"Nobody is Born Gay" Billboard Stuck Over Virginia Highway Until Next Year*, N.Y. DAILY NEWS, Dec. 11, 2014, *available at h*ttp://www.nydailynews.com/news/nationa/outrage-bord-gay-billboard-va-highway-article-1.2032203; Sarah Bloom, *"No One is Born Gay" Billboard Advertiser Responds to Controversy*, NBC12 (Dec. 12, 2014, 7:16 AM), http://www.nbc12.com/story/27589663/billboard-in-richmond-cliams-nobody-is-born-gay.

[13] *See* Laura Kebede, *Gay Community Center Group Portrait Planned to Counteract Billboard*, RICHMOND TIMES-

Another billboard of sorts, ironically, has caused a different kind of controversy in Charlottesville. When the Thomas Jefferson Center for the Protection of Free Expression and others in the city decided to erect some type of monument to free expression, they faced opposition. The monument was to be a seven-foot by 50-foot blackboard, upon which anyone could write anything at any time. Some citizens were afraid swear words and swastikas would appear on the blackboard. Others were worried about hate speech. Eventually the blackboard was approved.[14]

These last three cases are not examples of prior restraint. The restrictions – or potential restrictions – were caused, not by the government, but by individuals. Citizens feared either who was speaking or what the speech might be rather than of the content of specific speech. The examples, however, demonstrate that, at times, society can be as inhibiting of free speech as the government. Indeed, many efforts – successful and otherwise – to restrain speech never make it to court.

When cases do make it into Virginia courts, they have focused primarily on two types of prior restraint: (a) prohibitions against publishing specific types of information, that is, content-based prohibitions, and (b) restrictions on expressive conduct.

DISPATCH, Dec. 14, 2014, *available at* http://www.richmond.com/news/local/city-of-richmond/article_50a95cb4-9348-5e7a-8426-59FF0cfe412a.html.

[14] *See* Ellen Goodman, *In Charlottesville, a Monument to the Right of Free Speech,* ROANOKE TIMES, May 24, 2001, at A19.

CONTENT-BASED CENSORSHIP

Government entities in Virginia have frequently attempted to restrict expression on the basis of content. Most often, those efforts have been unsuccessful, but only because the U.S. Supreme Court has intervened. At least four times, beginning in the early 1970s, the U.S. Supreme Court has overturned efforts at censorship that courts in Virginia had allowed.

Prior Restraint From Richmond to Washington

In 1971, Jeffrey C. Bigelow was convicted of violating a Virginia statute making it illegal to encourage or promote the procurement of an abortion.[15] Bigelow, managing editor of the *Virginia Weekly* of Charlottesville, had published an advertisement for a New York abortion referral service. The ad did not specifically promote abortions, but noted that abortions were illegal in Virginia, but were legal in New York and were not restricted by residency requirements.[16]

Bigelow argued to the Virginia Supreme Court that he was not encouraging abortions, but was merely providing information for women who had decided not to carry their pregnancies to term.[17] The court upheld his conviction, however. First, the Virginia Supreme Court ruled, the language of the advertisement "constituted an active offer to perform a service, rather

---

[15] VA. CODE ANN. § 18.1-63 (1950).

[16] Bigelow v. Commonwealth, 191 S.E.2d 173 (Va. 1972), *rev'd* 421 U.S. 809 (1974). At the Supreme Court level the case is titled *Bigelow v. Virginia.*

[17] *Id.* at 174.

than a passive statement of fact."[18] Second, the court found that the statute did not violate the First Amendment of the Constitution, which was designed to protect the dissemination of information or opinion rather than commercial advertising, which the government can regulate.[19]

The U.S. Supreme Court disagreed. In *Bigelow v. Virginia,* the Court held that the advertisement contained information of interest to a diverse audience, and the fact that a service was being offered did not remove it from constitutional protection.[20] The Virginia statute, therefore, unconstitutionally infringed upon Bigelow's First Amendment rights.

Two years later, in *Virginia State Board of Pharmacy v. Virginia Citizens Consumer Council,*[21] the Court upheld a ruling by a three-judge panel of the Eastern District of Virginia[22] that a law prohibiting the advertisement of prescription drug prices was unconstitutional.[23] The listing of the drug prices, the Court held, was information consumers had a right to receive, and, therefore, it could not be restrained.[24]

Almost as if on schedule, in another two years, the Supreme Court once again ruled against Virginia. The case began as *Landmark Communications v.*

---

[18] *Id.*

[19] *Id.* at 175.

[20] 421 U.S. 809, 822 (1974).

[21] 425 U.S. 748 (1976).

[22] Virginia Citizens Consumer Council, Inc. v. State Bd. of Pharmacy, 373 F. Supp. 683 (E.D. Va. 1974).

[23] VA. CODE ANN. §54-524.35(3) (1950).

[24] 425 U.S. at 763-65.

Commonwealth.[25] The *Virginian-Pilot* of Norfolk published an article about an inquiry into possible disciplinary action against a judge by the state's Judicial Inquiry and Review Commission. State law prohibits the release of any information about hearings of the commission.[26] The *Virginian-Pilot* was convicted of violating the statute and fined $500.

Landmark Communications, which owns the *Virginian-Pilot,* argued to the Virginia Supreme Court that the statute involved unconstitutional prior restraint and that the state had not overcome the heavy presumption against the statute's constitutionality. Even if the statute did not restrain the press, Landmark argued, the state had failed to prove that the publication of the confidential proceedings caused a clear and present danger to the administration of justice.[27]

The state supreme court held that the statute did not constitute prior restraint, but provided for post-publication punishment.[28] And, the court held, there was ample evidence that publication of the confidential information from the commission would constitute a clear and present danger to the orderly administration of justice.[29]

Similar arguments were used in two cases that never reached the U.S. Supreme Court. In *Leonard v.*

---

[25] 233 S.E.2d 120 (Va. 1977), *rev'd* 435 U.S. 829 (1978). At the U.S. Supreme Court level the case is titled *Landmark Communications v. Virginia.*

[26] VA. CODE ANN. § 2.1-37.13 (1950).

[27] 233 S.E.2d at 124.

[28] *Id.*

[29] *Id.* at 129.

Fields[30] the federal court for the Western District of Virginia ruled that a sheriff had not acted improperly when he fired two deputies who, without permission, asked the Russell County Board of Supervisors for a three-cent mileage increase. Sheriff J. Trigg Fields said he considered the action of the deputies tantamount to mutiny, and the federal court ruled that the deputies were attempting to constitutionalize employee grievances by making First Amendment arguments.[31]

In *McBride v. Roanoke Redevelopment and Housing Authority*,[32] the same court held that the housing authority did not violate the free speech rights of its director by firing him for insensitive comments he made about the poor. The court held that the authority's legitimate interest in maintaining a favorable public perception outweighed the director's free speech rights. "A perception of the individual charged with overseeing the daily operations of the Authority as insensitive to the plight of the poor," the court held, "unquestionably would hinder the efficiency of the public services it provides – providing housing to low income individuals."[33]

It is unclear what would have happened if *Leonard* or *McBride* reached the U.S. Supreme Court, but in *Landmark Communications* the Court did not find persuasive arguments that the publication of information about the Judicial Inquiry and Review Commission would affect the efficiency of that agency. A news organization, the Court held, could

---

[30] 791 F. Supp. 143 (W.D. Va. 1992).

[31] *Id.* at 144.

[32] 871 F. Supp. 885 (W.D. Va. 1994).

[33] *Id.* at 893.

not be punished for the truthful publication of information about the conduct of public officials.[34] The commonwealth has a right to keep the information confidential, the Court noted, but once the information is in the hands of the press, there can be no punishment for the publication of that information.[35]

The U.S. Supreme Court nipped efforts by the commonwealth to censor information for the fourth time in 1996. The Court ruled that year that the University of Virginia unconstitutionally withheld funds from an organization that published a Christian-oriented newspaper. The university argued in *Rosenberger v. Rector and Trustees, University of Virginia*[36] that to provide the funds would violate the establishment clause of the First Amendment, but the Court held the action was content-based discrimination and, therefore, violated free-speech guarantees.

Wide Awake Productions was a student organization at the University of Virginia, but when the organization sought monies from the university's student activities funds to publish its newspaper, the funding was denied because the organization was religious. The U.S. District Court for the Western District of Virginia granted summary judgment for the university.[37] The Fourth U.S. Circuit Court of Appeals, though finding that the university's guidelines for disseminating student activities funds discriminated on the basis of content, affirmed the district court's ruling on grounds that the discrimination was justified by the compelling state

---

[34] 435 U.S. 829, 841-42 (1978).

[35] *Id.* at 840-41.

[36] 515 U.S. 819 (1995).

[37] 795 F. Supp. 175 (W.D. Va. 1992).

interest in maintaining strict separation between church and state.[38]

The Supreme Court disagreed. "It is axiomatic," the Court held, "that the government may not regulate speech based on its substantive content or the message it conveys."[39] That, the Court held, is exactly what happened to Wide Awake Productions.

The U.S. District Court for the Eastern District of Virginia found that the commonwealth misapplied the establishment clause in yet another case. In *Pruitt v. Wilder*[40] the court struck down a prohibition by the Virginia Department of Motor Vehicles on references to deities on personalized license plates.

Dan F. Pruitt wanted a license plate that read "GODZGUD," but was denied that plate because of a DMV policy statement prohibiting the issuance of license plates with references to "drug culture, lewd and obscene words, deities, or combinations which might otherwise be offensive."[41] References to deities, the court held, did not violate the establishment clause of the First Amendment, and the policy was a viewpoint-based regulation of speech, which violated that amendment.[42] Similarly, in 2012, a former Marine had his vanity license plate revoked because the Virginia Department of Motor Vehicles received complaints about his tag that said "ICUHAJI," which stands for "I see you haji."[43] This plate was

---

[38] 18 F.3d 269, 281 (4th Cir. 1994).

[39] 515 U.S. at 828.

[40] 840 F. Supp. 414 (E.D. Va. 1994).

[41] *Id.* at 415-16.

[42] *Id.* at 417-18.

[43] Bunjo v. Commonwealth, 86 Va. Cir. 32, 32 (Cir. Ct. 2012) (Chesapeake County).

considered by some as racist and offensive to Middle Easterners, and the Department of Motor Vehicles demanded the license plate's return. The Circuit Court of Chesapeake County deemed a state license plate as a non-public forum, and found that Department of Motor Vehicle's Guidelines unconstitutional because they were not viewpoint neutral.

The regulation of license plates garnered national attention when Governor Terry McAuliffe recalled Virginia license plates that contained Sons of Confederate Veterans logo. The SCV logo contained a predominant image of the Confederate battle flag. Litigation over Virginia's SCV license plates date back to 2001 when the SCV sued Virginia's motor vehicle commissioner alleging when he attempted to stop to issuance of SCV license plates. In that case, the U.S. District Court for the Western District of Virginia held that license plate logos did not represent the state's speech, but instead represented the speech of the individual license plate holder.[44] This holding was reaffirmed by the U.S. Court of Appeals for the Fourth Circuit in 2002.[45] However, the U.S. Supreme Court held in 2015 that states could disallow specialty license plates given that license plates represented the state's, not the individual holder's, speech.[46] In light of this decision, the U.S. District Court for the Western District of Virginia dissolved its 2001 injunction that

---

[44] Sons of Confederate Veterans, Inc. v. Holcomb, 129 F. Supp. 2d 941 (W.D. Va. 2001).

[45] Sons of Confederate Veterans, Inc. ex rel. Griffin v. Comm's of Va. Dep't of Motor Vehicles, 288 F.3d 610 (4th Cir. 2002), *reh'g denied* 305 F.3d 241 (4th Cir. 2002) (en banc).

[46] Walker v. Texas Div., Sons of Confederate Veterans, 135 S.Ct. 2239 (2015).

banned Virginia's Department of Motor Vehicles from treating SCV license plates differently from other specialty plates.[47]

State laws that limit a speaker's ability to profit from past misdeeds have also been constitutionally challenged. The Supreme Court, in effect, invalidated Virginia's "Son-of-Sam" statute in 1991 when it ruled that a similar statute from New York was unconstitutional.[48] Son-of-Sam statutes are named for New York mass murderer David Berkowitz, who signed notes about his murders as the "Son of Sam." When news circulated that Berkowitz was attempting to sell the rights to his story to book publishers, New York passed the first Son-of-Sam statute in the country in an attempt to prohibit criminals from profiting from stories about their crimes. Ironically, Berkowitz never profited from the book publication of the accounts of his murders, even though passage of New York's Son-of-Sam statute came too late to apply to him.[49] He was prohibited from profiting by state laws already in place. Nevertheless, many states passed similar statutes.

---

[47] Sons of Confederate Veterans Inc. v. Holcomb, No. 7:99-cv-00530, 2015 WL 4662435 (W.D. Va. Aug. 6, 2015).

[48] Simon & Schuster, Inc. v. New York Crime Victims Bd., 502 U.S. 105 (1991).

[49] For more on Son-of-Sam statutes, *see* Kerry Casey, Note, *The Virginia "Son of Sam" Law: An Unconstitutional Approach to Victim Compensation*, 2 WM. & MARY BILL RIGHTS 495 (1993); Sue S. Okuda, *Criminal Antiprofit Laws: Some Thoughts in Favor of Their Constitutionality,* 76 CALIF. L. REV. 1353 (1988); Jessica Yager, *Investigating New York's 2001 Son of Sam Law: Problems with the Recent Extension of Tort Liability for People Convicted of Crimes*, 48 N.Y.L. SCH. L. REV. 433 (2003-2004).

Virginia's law provides that no person convicted of a crime or found not guilty by reason of insanity may profit from any "movie, book, newspaper, magazine, radio or television production or live entertainment or publication of any kind," if "an integral part of the work is a depiction or discussion of the defendant's crime or an impression of the defendant's thoughts, opinions, or emotions" about the crime.[50] Any money earned by such expression must go into an escrow account for five years and be used to compensate victims of the person's crimes, to pay fines or to pay legal fees. At the end of the five years, the defendant can claim 25 percent of the remaining funds, with 25 percent going to the Criminal Injuries Compensation Fund.[51]

The New York law struck down by the U.S. Supreme Court had similar provisions. The Court held, however, that the law was a content-based restriction: "It singles out income derived from expressive activity for a burden the State places on no other income, and is directed only at works with a specific content."[52] The state, the Court noted, was unable to explain why it should have any greater interest in compensating victims from the proceeds of storytelling over any of a criminal's other assets. Nor was there any justification in distinguishing between the expressive activity of a criminal and any other "fruits of crime" the criminal may have earned.[53]

---

[50] VA. CODE ANN. § 19.2-368.20 (1950).

[51] VA. CODE ANN. § 19.2-368.21 (1950).

[52] *Simon & Schuster,* 502 U.S. at 116.

[53] *Id.* 119-20.

Virginia's Son-of-Sam law was more narrowly drawn than that of New York. In Virginia, a person must be convicted of a crime or found not guilty by reason of insanity before falling under the provisions of the law. In New York, a person need only confess to having committed a crime – and that confession might be found only in the expressive activity.

The distinction would likely have had little bearing on the Supreme Court's opinion, however. The Court's ruling was based, on the fact that the law discriminated on expressive activity. The Court found the New York statute unconstitutional because it was content-based. Virginia's statute, though more narrowly drawn, is also content-based because it regulates the subject matter of expressive activity.

Prior Restraint of Sexually Explicit Material

Sexually explicit material has been a source of controversy in many locales, and Virginia is no different. The commonwealth has made multiple efforts to restrict access to such material, some successful, some not. Courts have ruled, for example, that sexually explicit magazines can be withheld from prisoners, and that the commonwealth can restrict state employees from accessing sexually explicit Internet sites. On the other hand, a library was not allowed to install screening software on its computers, and a federal law prohibiting access to Web sites that contained material that might be harmful to children was found to be unconstitutional.

The U.S. District Court for the Western District of Virginia held that sexually explicit material could be withheld from prison inmates because the material had a negative impact on security, discipline, order, public safety and rehabilitation.[54] The U.S. Circuit Court of Appeals for the Fourth Circuit reversed that judgment on grounds that a company whose publication is restricted from prisoners must be given notice and the right to appeal, but did not address the finding that the material affected the operations of a prison.[55]

But, in a ruling that significantly limits the rights of state employees, the Fourth Circuit ruled in 1999 that the state may limit access to objectionable Web sites by state employees, even if the employees need access to those sites for research purposes.[56] In 1996, the general assembly passed a law restricting state employee access to Web sites containing sexually oriented material.[57] The law would allow access to such Web sites by a state employee if access was directly related to the employee's job and if the employee received permission from a supervisor. A group of university professors, with the assistance of the American Civil Liberties Union, sued to have the act declared unconstitutional, arguing that enforcement of the law would hamper their ability to conduct research. Research interests ranged from gender roles and sexuality to Victorian poets.

The U.S. District Court for the Eastern District of Virginia held that the law was unconstitutional.[58]

---

[54] Hodges v. Commonwealth, 871 F. Supp. 873, 877 (W.D. Va. 1994), *rev'd on other grounds,* Montcalm Publ'g Corp. v. Beck, 80 F.3d 105 (4th Cir. 1996).

[55] *Montcalm,* 80 F.3d at 109.

[56] Urofsky v. Gilmore, 167 F.3d 191 (4th Cir. 1999).

[57] VA. CODE ANN. §§ 2.1-804 - 805 (1950).

[58] Urofsky v. Allen, 995 F. Supp. 634 (E.D. Va. 1998). The name of the case changed because the suit was filed when

The court recognized that the government, in some circumstances, could restrict the speech of employees, but also recognized that there is both an individual and societal interest in free speech activities of government employees. Those interests, the court said, must be balanced against the government's interest in restricting the speech.[59] When the government restrictions are based on content, the court added, the government must demonstrate a compelling interest and the restrictions must be narrowly tailored to meet that interest.[60]

The provision that access to sexually explicit material may be approved only "to the extent required in conjunction with a bona fide, agency-approved research project" makes the act even more obnoxious, the court held. The restriction allows agencies, rather than employees, to determine the types of research required by employees as well as the type of research that is bona fide.[61] The court also noted that a number of content-neutral alternatives already existed to accommodate the problems about which the government is concerned.[62]

The Fourth Circuit reversed the decision. The court found significant the distinction between speech made by a person acting primarily as a citizen and speech made by a person acting primarily as a state employee. The employees were making the claim, the

---

George Allen was governor of Virginia (1994-1998), and Jim Gilmore replaced Allen as governor in 1999.

[59] *Id.* at 636.

[60] *Id.* at 637.

[61] *Id.* at 641-42.

[62] *Id.* at 643.

court held, that they were entitled to access in their capacity as state employees, so they could not simultaneously claim that the access was related to their capacity as citizens involved in speech on matters of public concern. Therefore, because the regulation limited the speech of state employees in their capacity as employees and because the state had the right to retain the ability to control the manner in which its employees discharge their duties, the regulation was constitutional.[63]

In yet another cyberspace case, a policy by which the Loudoun County Library installed software on its computers intended to block Web sites containing child pornography or obscene material was held by the federal district court for the Eastern District of Virginia to be unconstitutional.[64] Applying the strict scrutiny test, the court found that protecting patrons from sexual harassment was a compelling government interest, but that the policy was not narrowly tailored to meet that interest.[65] The court also found the policy to be infirm because it was devoid of standards by which a reviewing authority could determine if the blocking decisions were appropriate.[66]

But, in 2011, the U.S. Supreme Court held that mandatory Internet filters in public libraries did not violate the First Amendment. The case involved the constitutionality of the Children's Internet Protection

---

[63] 167 F.3d 191, 196 (4th Cir. 1999).

[64] Mainstream Loudoun v. Bd. of Trustees of the Loudoun Cty. Library, 24 F. Supp. 2d 552 (E.D. Va. 1998).

[65] *Id.* at 565-67.

[66] *Id.* at 569.

Act, passed in 2000, which required public libraries to use an Internet filter system for pornography. Access to the Internet in public libraries is largely the consequence of federal funding. However, prior to the passage of CIPA, libraries noted that library patrons, including children, were using free library Internet to access pornographic and obscene materials. After Congress passed CIPA, public libraries receiving federal funding had to use Internet filters that blocked obscene and pornographic material. A group of libraries challenged the CIPA alleging that mandatory Internet blocks violated the First Amendment. They specifically argued that CIPA blocked more than obscene or pornographic material including literary, medical and scientific Web sites. Citing Congress' ability to attach conditions to federal funding, the U.S. Supreme Court held in a plurality opinion that Internet access is not a public or designated public forum. Because of this Congress' requirement that libraries receiving federal funding use Internet filter is constitutional even if the filter software blocks fully protected Internet content. [67]

The protection of minors from obscene or pornographic material does have limits. In 2004, the Fourth Circuit, in a case out of the Western District of Virginia, had problems with a Virginia criminal statute that restricted Internet use. The law criminalized the displaying of Internet content that was potentially harmful to minors.[68] In that case, the Fourth Circuit

---

[67] United States v. American Library Ass'n., 539 U.S. 194 (2003).

[68] VA. CODE ANN. § 18.2-391 (Michie Supp. 1999). This law first applied to stores and retailers. It was changed in 1999 and again in 2000 to apply specifically to online content. The

found unconstitutional a Virginia law that prohibited sexually explicit content that minors could potentially access online. The court found that even though the government could show a compelling interest in the law, the statute was unconstitutional because it was not narrowly tailored. The overbreadth of the law created a vague standard to identify prohibited content and content that is fully protected under the First Amendment. The law was also flawed in that it only applied to commercial sites and could not effectively be enforced against non-Virginia citizens.[69]

Other Restrictions

Not all restrictions on expression are designed to inhibit the dissemination of information and ideas. Indeed, some restrictions are designed to promote an understanding of issues important to the public. Virginia law contains several restrictions that fall into this category. For example, state law makes it illegal for a person to knowingly give a news organization false information for the purpose of publication or broadcast,[70] and any person from attaching to a newspaper any communication that was not authorized by the publisher.[71]

Spam has also been an issue within the Virginia courts. In 2003, President George W. Bush signed the CAN-SPAM Act, which set requirements for and allowed federal regulation of bulk emails.[72] As a

---

Fourth Circuit found an earlier version of the law constitutional in 1985. *See* American Booksellers Ass'n v. Virginia, 882 F.2d 125 (4th Cir. 1989).

[69] PSINET v. Chapman, 362 F.3d 227 (4th Cir. 2004).

[70] VA. CODE ANN. § 18.2-209 (1950).

[71] VA. CODE ANN. § 18.2-210 (1950).

[72] 15 U.S.C. §§ 7701-7713 (2003).

result, states, including Virginia, passed statutes that also regulated bulk emails. In 2008, however, the Virginia Supreme Court struck down Virginia's anti-spam law.[73] The law criminalized sending false or forged bulk emails to more than 10,000 accounts within 24 hours, 100,000 within 30 days, or one million within one year. The Court, however, held that the law was unconstitutional because it did not differentiate between types of email correspondence.[74]

The case involved Jeremy Jaynes, a Raleigh, North Carolina, citizen, who emailed spam on a regular basis. In his possession were millions of email addresses and more than 1.3 billion user names he acquired from a former AOL employee. Although he sent his emails from North Carolina, Jaynes was charged in Virginia under the anti-spam statute. Jaynes's conviction was upheld by the Virginia Court of Appeals, but the Virginia Supreme Court reversed. In its opinion, the court found that the Virginia anti-spam statute was unconstitutional under the First Amendment because it was overly broad. Specifically, the court cited the statute's lack of specificity of email type. Under Virginia's 2003 anti-spam statute, all emails – commercial, non-commercial, illegal and legal – were banned. Virginia appealed the state supreme court's decision to U.S. Supreme Court but *certiorari* was denied.[75] In 2010, Virginia re-wrote portions of the statute to be more specific, and

---

[73] VA. CODE ANN. § 18.2-152.3:1 (1950).

[74] Jaynes v. Commonwealth, 666 S.E.2d 303 (Va. 2008), *cert denied*, 556 U.S. 1152 (2009).

[75] Virginia v. Jaynes, 556 U.S. 1152 (2009).

included language that limited the statute's application to purpose and content of the prohibited emails.[76]

RESTRICTIONS ON EXPRESSIVE CONDUCT

A variety of types of expressive conduct – from selling magazine subscriptions, to marching, to burning crosses and flags – have come under attack in Virginia. Most efforts at suppression, however, have been ruled unconstitutional.

Even the state supreme court, which, as has been demonstrated, is not known for granting broad protection to expression, has been hesitant in restricting expressive conduct. In 1948, the Virginia Supreme Court held, "The Constitution of Virginia is broader than that of the United States in providing that 'any citizen may freely speak, write and publish his sentiments on all subjects.'"[77] However, the court noted in 2004 that this statement on expansiveness is merely *dicta*, and that Article 1 section 12 of the Virginia Constitution "is coextensive with the free speech provisions of the federal First Amendment."[78] And the court defined "publishing" as bringing information before the public for sale or distribution.[79]

In addition, the court has ruled that "the streets and highways belong to the public." Since they are "natural and proper places for the dissemination of information and opinion by citizens," they cannot be regulated in a manner that restricts free expression.[80]

---

[76] VA. CODE Ann. § 18.2-152.3:1 (1950).

[77] Robert v. Norfolk, 49 S.E.2d 697, 700 (Va. 1948).

[78] Elliott v. Commonwealth, O'Mara v. Commonwealth, 593 S.E. 2d 263, 269 (Va. 2004).

[79] *Robert*, 49 S.E.2d at 700.

[80] *Id.*

An ordinance prohibiting the door-to-door solicitation of magazine subscriptions without a license, therefore, was held to be unconstitutional.

Similarly, the court has held that citizens have a right to march, parade or demonstrate on public streets.[81] Towns and cities may impose reasonable time, place and manner restrictions and may require parade permits, but those permits may not be arbitrarily refused and may not be refused based upon the nature or content of the demonstration. And potential marchers may not be required to meet unreasonable criteria before being granted the permits.[82] However, it is important to note that the Virginia Supreme Court has long held that trespass statutes apply equally to property owned by individuals and the commonwealth.[83]

Courts are generally more willing to protect private property from individuals or groups making free speech arguments. The Virginia Supreme Court held, for example, that the state constitution does not allow a person to distribute information on private property once that person is ordered to stay off the property.[84] By statute, Virginia also prohibits the picketing of a private residence, unless certain requirements are met.[85] And, the Fourth Circuit has

---

[81] York v. Danville, 152 S.E.2d 259, 263 (Va. 1967).

[82] *Id.* at 263-64.

[83] *See* Johnson v. Virginia, 186 S.E.2d 53 (Va. 1972); Miller v. Harless, 149 S.E. 619 (1929).

[84] Hall v. Commonwealth, 49 S.E.2d 369 (Va.1948).

[85] VA. CODE ANN. § 18.2-419 (1950). Picketing of a labor dispute, construction site or a place wherein a meeting on a topic of general public interest is occurring are allowed, even if private dwelling places are involved.

held that the Freedom to Access to Clinic Entrances Act of 1994, which prohibits protestors from obstructing access to abortion clinics, is constitutional.[86] The act, the court held, does not prohibit protesting, the distribution of handbills and other forms of expression, so long as the activities are carried out in a non-violent, non-obstructive manner and physical obstruction or threat of force is not used to interfere with a person's right to enter the clinics.[87]

The state supreme court has also held that noise ordinances are unconstitutional if they are aimed at restraining controversial speech which, by its nature, may upset the peace and tranquility of the community.[88] The government may restrain efforts to incite riots or the participation in riots, but may not restrain speech simply because the speech may cause unrest due to its uncomfortable or obnoxious nature.[89]

The court also ruled that Virginia's unlawful assembly ordinance is unconstitutionally overbroad.[90] The case began when demonstrators in Charlottesville were arrested after refusing to disperse as ordered by law enforcement officers. The court held that the statute, in addition to punishing genuine disturbances of the peace, would punish peaceful gatherings for purposes protected by the First Amendment. The

---

[86] American Life League, Inc. v. Reno, 47 F.3d 642 (4th Cir. 1995).

[87] *Id.* at 648.

[88] Thomas v. Danville, 152 S.E.2d 265, 270 (Va. 1967).

[89] *Id.*

[90] Owens v. Commonwealth, Ferguson v. Commonwealth, 179 S.E.2d 477 (Va. 1971). The unlawful assembly statute, VA. CODE Ann. § 18.1-254.1 (1950), was repealed in 1975.

ordinance, therefore, was unconstitutional, and a conviction for its violation could not stand.[91]

Virginia's law prohibiting mutilation of the flag is probably unconstitutional as well, though there has been no ruling on the statute. In 1989, the U.S. Supreme Court struck down as unconstitutional the Texas flag-desecration law, which was very similar to Virginia's.[92]

Virginia, in fact, has two statutes aimed at protecting the U.S. and Virginia flags. One statute prohibits flying a flag that has been altered in any way,[93] while a second states that "[n]o person shall publicly burn with contempt, mutilate, deface, defile, trample upon, or wear with intent to defile any such flag, standard, color, ensign or shield."[94]

The U.S. Supreme Court held in the Texas case that burning a flag as a sign of dissatisfaction with governmental policies was protected political speech. A year later, the Court reiterated that point in striking down the newly adopted Flag Protection Act.[95] Since Virginia's law is aimed at the suppression of speech, it is probably unconstitutional as well.

Virginia legislators have recognized that some forms of expressive conduct are designed to frighten or intimidate people and have taken steps to prohibit those acts. Three statutes, in particular, are designed to prohibit the use of recognized symbols for purposes of intimidation. One of the statutes was held by the

---

[91] *Id.* at 481.

[92] Texas v. Johnson, 491 U.S. 397 (1989).

[93] VA. CODE Ann. § 18.2-487 (1950).

[94] VA. CODE Ann. § 18.2-488 (1950).

[95] United States v. Eichmann, 496 U.S. 310 (1990).

Supreme Court to be unconstitutional, though the portion of the statute struck down by the Court has been revised and, apparently, remains intact.

Barry Black was convicted of burning a cross at a Ku Klux Klan rally in Carroll County August 22, 1998,[96] in violation of a state law that prohibited such an action "with the intent of intimidating any person or group of persons."[97] He was fined $2,500,[98] and the conviction was affirmed by the Virginia Court of Appeals.[99] Black's case was joined with two other cross-burning cases, *O'Mara v. Commonwealth* and *Elliott v. Commonwealth.*[100] Richard Elliott had indicated unspecified complaints with James Jubilee, and Jonathan S. O'Mara offered to help him burn a cross in Jubilee's yard. The Virginia Supreme Court found the statute unconstitutional because it was a content-based regulation that was overbroad.[101]

The U.S. Supreme Court affirmed the holding, but for different reasons.[102] Virginia's law established that the very fact that a person burned a cross would be *prima facie* evidence that the person intended to intimidate someone. That is, as Justice Sandra Day O'Connor wrote for the Court, "[P]resentation of evidence that a defendant burned a cross in public

---

[96] Black v. Commonwealth, 553 S.E.2d 738, 741 (Va. 2000).

[97] VA. CODE Ann. § 18.2-423 (1950).

[98] *Black*, 553 S.E.2d at 741.

[99] Black v. Commonwealth, 535 S.E.2d 115 (Va. App. 2000).

[100] 535 S.E.2d 175 (Va. App. 2000).

[101] *Black*, 553 S.E.2d at 745-46.

[102] Virginia v. Black, 538 U.S. 343 (2003).

view is automatically sufficient, on its own, to support an inference that the defendant intended to intimidate."[103] Therefore, the defendant would be required to produce evidence of innocence, which violates the Constitution. Justice O'Connor found that there are many types of cross burning, and not all are intended to intimidate.

The cross-burning statute remains on the books, but the reference in the statute to any burning of a cross being *prima facie* evidence of intent to intimidate has been eliminated. The statute reads:

> It shall be unlawful for any person or persons, with the intent of intimidating any person or group of persons, to burn, or cause to be burned, a cross on the property of another, a highway or other public place. Any person who shall violate ay provision of this section shall be guilty of a Class 6 felony.[104]

Virginia's swastika law, however, is not as broad as the cross-burning statute. The law prohibits the placing of a swastika in order to intimidate any person or group, but only prohibits the placement of the swastika on a place of worship or on an educational facility or community center owned by a religious body.[105] The law has not been challenged, but the law,

---

[103] *Id.* at 371.

[104] VA. CODE Ann. § 18.2-423 (1950). After the U.S. Supreme Court's decision in *Black v. Virginia*, the Virginia Supreme Court affirmed the convictions of Elliott and O'Mara. *See* Elliott v. Commonwealth, O'Mara v. Commonwealth, 593 S.E.2d 263 (Va. 2004).

[105] VA. CODE Ann. § 18.2-433.1 (1950).

like the St. Paul cross-burning statute, is aimed at protecting a particular class of people – those who are members of organized religions.

Similarly, a federal court has upheld as constitutional Virginia's ordinance prohibiting an adult from wearing a mask except in certain circumstances.[106] The court held that a mask worn as part of Ku Klux Klan regalia did not convey a particularized message apart from the remainder of the costume and contributed nothing to the message already conveyed, so First Amendment rights were not infringed.[107]

ABUSIVE LANGUAGE

At times, abusive language can almost take on the role of conduct. If language is aimed at an individual, for example, and is so offensive that it is likely to cause the individual to respond with physical violence, the language falls into that category of speech the U.S. Supreme Court has called "fighting words" and is not protected.[108]

Virginia law prohibits fighting words and certain other classes of abusive language from being uttered in both face-to-face contexts and over the airwaves. Both statutes have been held to be

---

[106] VA. CODE Ann. § 18.2-422 (1950). A mask can be worn as part of a holiday costume, as part of a person's professional attire, as part of a theatrical production or for medical reasons.

[107] Hernandez v. Superintendent, Fredericksburg-Rappahonnock Joint Sec. Ctr., 800 F. Supp. 1344, 1351 (E.D. Va. 1992).

[108] Chaplinsky v. New Hampshire, 315 U.S. 568 (1942).

constitutional by Virginia courts, but for different reasons.

Virginia prohibits a person from cursing or abusing another person with language "reasonably calculated to provoke a breach of the peace."[109] The statute has been held to apply only to fighting words, that is, words that would have a direct tendency to cause acts of violence;[110] if remarks are not made in a face-to-face confrontation, the statute does not apply. The Virginia Court of Appeals, therefore, held that abusive language made in an argument between two neighbors was not actionable because the neighbors were separated by at least 55 feet and a chain-link fence.[111]

Under that rationale, it may seem that the same court should also find that the Virginia statute prohibiting the use of profane, threatening or indecent language over the public airwaves, including telephone lines, is unconstitutional.[112] After all, there can be no face-to-face confrontation in such circumstances. The court, however, found just the opposite. In *Parker v. Commonwealth* the Virginia Court of Appeals held that Virginia's stalking law was neither unconstitutionally vague nor was overly broad even though the statute outlaws all behavior that makes victims have "reasonable fear of death."[113] The

---

[109] VA. CODE Ann. § 18.2-416 (1950).

[110] Mercer v. Winston, 199 S.E.2d 724 (Va. 1973).

[111] Hershfield v. Commonwealth, 417 S.E.2d 876 (Va. App. 1992).

[112] VA. CODE Ann. §18.2-427 (1950).

[113] VA. CODE Ann. §18.2-60.3 (1950).

Virginia Court of Appeals held that repeatedly making threatening phone calls by telephone was a form of stalking, that is, was conduct rather than speech.[114] The legislature intended for the law to address harassing conduct, the court found, and ruled that, as applied, "it proscribes conduct and not speech."[115]

[114] Parker v. Commonwealth, 485 S.E.2d 150 (Va. Ct. App. 1997).

[115] Perkins v. Commonwealth, 402 S.E.2d 229, 233 (Va. Ct. App. 1991).

4. CYBERSPACE LAW IN VIRGINIA

New technology has always had an impact on the law. With the dawn of radio came regulations of the airwaves. The introduction of television spawned regulations on advertising, content and media ownership. The growth of the Internet and social media in the past decade is no different. It has caused the law to be reconsidered and reevaluated while well-established principles are preserved.

In Virginia, as in the rest of the United States, the law is based on common law, that is, court decisions of the past, and modern statutes. With the introduction of new technologies, these older legal principles must adapt. The challenge for courts and legislatures is to adapt older, well-established legal principles to the modern technological age. Law and technology interact in unique and complex ways. Technology frequently leads to new interpretations and application of older laws. Law, in turn, sometimes struggles to keep up with technological innovation.

Despite these complex relationships, new technology does not change age-old legal principles. Rather, the technologies must operate within a legal system that has been in existence since the ratification of the U.S. Constitution. However, the digital age has created new scenarios unanticipated by current laws. The growth of globalized communication, the proliferation of personal information online, and social media have created new communication and legal realities.

Virginia law, like that in the other 49 states, struggles to keep up with these changes.

JURISDICTIONAL ISSUES WITH CYBERSPACE

Cyberspace is a global phenomenon. Because of that, deciding which type of jurisdiction is proper for a lawsuit can be difficult. American jurisdiction essentially can be divided into two areas. The first is subject matter jurisdiction. The question to be asked is, "Where is the proper court to bring this type of lawsuit?" For instance, if a person wanted to bring a lawsuit regarding a trademark issue, then the proper court would be federal. That is because federal courts, not state, have subject matter jurisdiction over trademarks. Subject matter jurisdiction is given to a court because the underlying issue is based on federal or state law. Other times subject matter jurisdiction is given to specialized courts, such as U.S. Bankruptcy Courts, because those courts have a specialized expertise in a particular legal issue.[1]

The second type of jurisdiction is personal jurisdiction. The question to be asked is, "Where can I sue a particular person or entity."[2] Usually this is answered by determining where a person or entity resides. For instance, if a person wanted to bring a lawsuit for damages in excess of $10,000 against a Virginia corporation with headquarters in Richmond, personal jurisdiction over that company would be in Virginia Circuit Court in Richmond. However, it is not enough to just have subject matter or personal jurisdiction over a defendant. The court where a

---

[1] *See* VA. CONST. art. 6 §1; 28 U.S.C. §1332 (2000); VA. CODE ANN. §16.1-77 (1950). A more complete discussion of Virginia courts in found in Chapter 2.

[2] *See* 28 U.S.C. §1391 (2000); VA. CODE ANN. §8.01-328.1 (1950); World-Wide Volkswagen Corp. v. Woodson, 444 U.S. 286 (1980).

defendant is sued must have both subject matter and personal jurisdiction over the case.[3]

Cyberspace complicates this formula because online legal issues can occur in multiple jurisdictions both within the United States and internationally. For instance, a person sending a computer virus from a computer in California can affect computers worldwide. This presents several questions. Would that sender be subject to jurisdiction in every state or country his virus appears? What if those jurisdictions have differing laws regarding computer viruses? Can those laws apply to a person who has never physically been to any of the locations where the virus occurred? As this hypothetical demonstrates jurisdictional questions about cyberspace issues can become complex and frequently do not have clear answers.

Global Jurisdictional Issues

Jurisdictional issues in cyberspace are more important than where a plaintiff can properly sue a defendant. Cyber-jurisdictional issues are about sovereignty, or the right of a country or state to legally govern itself. There is power in being able to hold an individual legally accountable for his or her actions in court. Because of this, there have been jurisdictional fights over whether American citizens or companies can be legally held accountable in foreign courts. These courts may or may not have the same rights for legal parties. One country may criminalize behavior

---

[3] For more information about jurisdiction in the United States, *see* Paul Gugliuzza, *Rethinking Federal Circuit Jurisdiction*, 100 GEORGETOWN L.J. 1437 (2012); Allan Trammell & Derek Bambauer, *Personal Jurisdiction and the "Interwebs,"* 100 CORNELL L. REV. 1129 (2015).

that is perfectly legal in another, which causes a problem for those using an international platform such as the World Wide Web.[4]

One example of a jurisdictional conflict over a foreign national in a cyberspace case arose during 2001 when the U.S. Department of Justice brought criminal charges against Jay Cohen, a derivatives trader turned Caribbean bookmaker. Cohen advertised heavily in the United States, soliciting participation for his online gambling business based in the Caribbean. Even though Cohen's bookmaking business was operated legally in the island of Antigua, his solicitations and his online betting parlors heavily targeted the United States. Because solicitation for online gambling purposes was illegal in the United States,[5] Cohen was convicted and sentenced to twenty-one months in prison.[6]

Outside of the United States, the European Union has begun to enforce its so-called "right to be forgotten" laws on search engines that operate outside of the E.U. Right-to-be-forgotten laws essentially give individuals the right to demand removal of certain online content concerning themselves from search engine results. While this type of law would be unconstitutional in the United States, companies

---

[4] International jurisdiction in cyberspace issues is a complex area of law that affects Europe and the United States. *See, e.g.,* Ray August, *International Cyber Jurisdiction: A Comparative Analysis*, 39 AMER. BUS. L. J. 531 (2002).

[5] 18 U.S.C. §1084 (2000).

[6] United States v. Cohen, 260 F.3d 68 (2d Cir. 2001). *See also,* United States v. Cohen, 128 Fed. Appx. 825 (2d Cir. 2005).

operating in the United States are affected by this E.U. law.[7]

Virginia Jurisdiction Over Cyberspace

Jurisdictional issues in cyberspace lawsuits are a bit more clear-cut in Virginia jurisdictions. The Virginia Code presents 10 ways in which a person or entity can be subject to personal jurisdiction in Virginia's courts. Among these are conducting business in the commonwealth, causing injury to another in the commonwealth, and owning property in the commonwealth.[8] These 10 ways stem from a person or the actions by a person's agent within or toward Virginia or its citizens. These actions are very important because they include actions made online.

Frequently referred to as a "long arm" statute, the Virginia's personal jurisdiction code allows jurisdiction over people or entities that have some type of contact with Virginia or its citizens.[9] The power of this type of personal jurisdiction is that Virginia courts can have jurisdiction over out-of-state residents and businesses. These long arm statutes are particularly applicable to online activities. According to the Virginia Code, certain online activities give Virginia

---

[7] For more information about the European Union and the so-called "right to be forgotten," *see* Jane Kirtley, *"Misguided in Principle and Unworkable in Practice": It is Time to Discard the* Reporters Committee *Doctrine of Practical Obscurity (and Its Evil Twin, the Right to be Forgotten),* 20 COMM. L. & POL'Y 91 (2015); Cayce Myers, *Digital Immortality vs. "The Right to be Forgotten": A Comparison of U.S. and E.U. Laws Concerning Social Media Privacy*, 16 ROMANIAN J. OF COMM. AND PUB. REL. 47 (2014).

[8] VA. CODE ANN. § 8.01-328.1 (1950).

[9] *Id.*

courts personal jurisdiction over individuals or organizations whose actions affect residents of Virginia. The power of the statute is found in its definitions of online behavior. The statute states personal jurisdiction exists when a person or organization is "using a computer or computer network located in the Commonwealth."[10] The term "computer network" has a broad meaning under Virginia law. A "computer network" exists when "two or more computers [are] connected by a network."[11] More importantly, computer "use" in Virginia means, "[W]hen [a person or organization] attempts to cause or causes a computer or computer network to perform or to stop performing computer operations."[12] As expected "computer operations" also has a broad definition that includes: "[A]rithmetic, logical, monitoring, storage or retrieval functions and any combination thereof, and includes, but is not limited to, communication with, storage of data to, or retrieval of data from any device or human hand manipulation of electronic or magnetic impulses."[13]

These definitions are important because within the statutory construction of Virginia's long arm computer statute there is wide latitude for Virginia courts to assert personal jurisdiction over out-of-state defendants who engage in cyberspace activities. This is evident in what courts have done, specifically in

---

[10] VA. CODE ANN. § 8.01-328.1(B) (1950).
[11] VA. CODE ANN. §18.2-152.2 (1950).
[12] VA. CODE ANN. §18.2-152.2(4)(1950).
[13] VA. CODE ANN. §18.2-152.2 (1950).

regard to out-of-state defendants who send emails to Virginia residents.[14]

However, just because a person's online activities may have an affect in Virginia, that does not mean there is automatically personal jurisdiction over that person. To have personal jurisdiction there must be a requisite amount of contact within the commonwealth. Frequently referred to as "minimum contacts," courts examine the amount and intentionality of a defendant's contact with Virginia. The circuit court in Fairfax County held that an Internet seller on eBay was not subject to personal jurisdiction in the commonwealth even though he sold a car online to a Virginia resident. The court reasoned that because the seller "did not 'manifest an intent to target and focus on Virginia' buyers" in his eBay listing, personal jurisdiction did not exist.[15]

The minimum contacts standard in personal jurisdiction is very fact sensitive. *The Hartford Courant* and the *New Haven Advocate* in Connecticut were sued by a Virginia prison warden for defamation. The warden claimed the papers portrayed him as a racist in two online articles about Virginia prisons. The U.S. Court of Appeals for the Fourth Circuit, analyzing the Virginia long-arm statute, held personal jurisdiction over the Connecticut newspapers did not exist in Virginia because the newspapers did not have minimum contacts with the state. The Fourth Circuit reasoned that merely placing an article on the Internet

---

[14] *See* Atkins v. Commc'ns. Workers of America, 496 F. Supp. 2d 653 (E.D. Va. 2007); Jaynes v. Commonwealth, 666 S.E.2d 303 (Va. 2008).

[15] Irving v. Wagner Zone, Inc. 68 Va. Cir. 127, 129 (Cir. Ct. 2005) (Fairfax County) (citing Young v. New Haven Advocate, 315 F.3d 256, 263 (4th Cir. 2002)).

that may be read in Virginia did not constitute the contacts required for personal jurisdiction.[16]

However, a person is still subject to personal jurisdiction in Virginia if he or she carries out a criminal activity that results in injury in Virginia. In *Jaynes v. Commonwealth,* the Supreme Court of Virginia held that a defendant who operated an out-of-state computer spam system was still subject to personal jurisdiction in Virginia because his crimes were carried out in the commonwealth.[17] However, mere association with an online criminal enterprise does not constitute personal jurisdiction in Virginia. The federal court for the Eastern District of Virginia held that Virginia courts had no personal jurisdiction over banks that served as credit card processors for an online pharmaceutical scam. The scam involved two Russian citizens who posed as an online Canadian pharmacy and processed online orders through four banks. The court held that asserting personal jurisdiction over the banks when they had no contacts with Virginia nor made any attempt at doing so would violate their due process rights.[18]

---

[16] Young v. New Haven Advocate, 315 F.3d 256 (4th Cir. 2002), *cert. denied,* 538 U.S. 1035 (2003).

[17] 666 S.E.2d 303 (Va. 2008). *See also* Traveler's Health Ass'n. v. Commonwealth, 51 S.E.2d 263 (Va. 1949).

[18] Project Honey Pot v. John Does, No. 1:11CV15 (LMB/JFA), 2012 WL 1854184 (E.D. Va. May 21, 2012). Due process in this case stands for the idea that the government cannot deprive a person of "life, liberty, or property without the due process of law." The due process guarantees are found in both the Fifth and Fourteenth Amendments of the U.S. Constitution.

Access to Online Content

The growth of the Internet and social media means that much more personal information is online, an issue addressed by Virginia law in two ways. First, Virginia has developed specific laws concerning the subpoenaing of online content. Second, the Virginia legislature enacted new statutory protections that forbid employer access to workers' social media accounts.

Subpoenas for Online Information

Computer information may be subpoenaed as evidence for both criminal and civil cases. A subpoena is a writ that compels individuals either to present themselves or, as is the case with a subpoena duces tecum, produce documentary or physical evidence. Subpoenas are quite powerful, but recipients often challenge them. In cases involving cyberspace evidence, subpoenas are even used to uncover anonymous identities. That issue involves both a plaintiff's right to uncover evidence and speaker's right to remain anonymous.

Virginia courts addressed anonymous online speech rights in the late 1990s. In 1999, a publically traded company headquartered in Indiana subpoenaed American Online to reveal the identities of five anonymous posters of online content who resided in Virginia. These anonymous posters wrote negative reviews of the company, and the company wanted to sue for defamation. Because the users who posted the comments were anonymous, the only means the Indiana company had to uncover their identities was to subpoena AOL. Fearing that its business would receive negative publicity, AOL fought the subpoena, alleging that revealing the identities of the users constituted a violation of their First Amendment rights.[19] The Virginia Circuit Court in Fairfax County adopted a three-prong test to determine when a subpoena forces ISPs to disclose anonymous users' identities. The court held that ISPs must comply with the subpoena if:

> (1) the court is satisfied by the pleadings or evidence supplied to that court;
> (2) the party requesting the subpoena has a legitimate, good faith basis to contend that it may be the victim of conduct actionable in the jurisdiction where suit was filed, and
> (3) the subpoenaed identity information is centrally needed to advance that claim.[20]

This test places a burden on the plaintiff to make a prima facie case. The inherent problem is that without the identity of a defendant gathering evidence to support a claim is very difficult. However, despite this burden, the circuit court denied AOL's motion to quash the subpoena.

AOL appealed the circuit court's decision to the Virginia Supreme Court, challenging the Indiana

---

[19] The U.S. Supreme Court's approach to anonymous speech is complex. The Court affirmed the right to keep membership lists private in *NAACP v. Alabama*, 357 U.S. 449 (1958), and held that anonymous speech is an important component to the First Amendment in *McIntyre v. Ohio Election Commission*, 514 U.S. 334 (1995). For an extensive analysis of anonymity's role within the First Amendment, s*ee McIntyre v. Ohio Election Commission,* 514 U.S 334, 359-68 (1995)(Thomas, J., concurring).

[20] In re Subpoena Duces Tecum to America Online, 52 Va. Cir. 26, 37 (Cir. Ct. 2000) (Fairfax County).

company's right to remain anonymous. The Indiana company seeking the subpoena was kept anonymous in all the Virginia court decisions regarding the subpoena of the anonymous AOL users. AOL argued that the Indiana company should not be allowed to proceed anonymously while also using Virginia courts to enforce a subpoena *duces tecum.* The Virginia Supreme Court ultimately agreed, but did not rule on the merits of the Fairfax County Circuit Court's approach to assessing subpoenas seeking to uncover anonymous online speakers.[21] Although the circuit courts of Virginia do not set precedent for the entire commonwealth, this approach is constitutionally valid and has been considered in jurisdictions outside Virginia.[22]

AOL challenged another subpoena duces tecum involving online content in 2008 in federal court for the Eastern District of Virginia. That case dealt with the issuance of a subpoena for emails from the account of two non-party witnesses in an insurance fraud case. The subpoena duces tecum was challenged as a violation of the federal Privacy Act[23] and as being overly broad for seeking privileged information. The federal court agreed, holding that the subpoena was in violation of the Privacy Act and was overly broad. Specifically, the court held that a request for emails for six weeks without specifying the topic of those emails

---

[21] America Online, Inc. v. Anonymous Public Traded Co., 542 S.E.2d 377 (Va. 2001).

[22] For other approaches to subpoena duces tecum and anonymous users, *see* Cahill v. John Doe No. One, 879 A.2d 943 (Del. Super. 2005), *rev'd* John Doe No. 1 v. Cahill, 884 A.2d 451 (Del. 2005); Dendrite Int'l. v. John Doe, No. 3, 775 A.2d 756 (N.J. Super. 2001).

[23] 18 U.S.C. §2701 (2000).

constituted an overly broad request that had the potential to include privileged information.[24]

Social Media and Employment Law

Social media have created a new reality for many workers in America. Because of the amount of personal information available there, employers have used social media to screen job applicants, monitor employee speech, and even as justification for termination. In response, there has been a push for greater protection of employee speech on social media. In 2012, the National Labor Relations Board ruled that social media speech could contain legitimate workplace grievances protected by the National Labor Relations Act.[25] As a result of that ruling, businesses making certain social media speech a fireable offense were barred from doing so.[26]

Several states have passed laws that forbid employers from asking job applicants for access to their social media accounts. The laws were in response to many job applicants having to turn over social media access as part of their job interviews. In July 2015, Virginia passed a statute specifically outlining the social media rights of employees and job

---

[24] In re Subpoena Duces Tecum to AOL, LLC, 550 F. Supp. 2d 606 (E.D. Va. 2008). The judge declined to rule on the privilege issue because the lawsuit was filed in an out-of-state federal court.

[25] Hispanics United of Buffalo, 359 NLRB No. 37 (Dec. 14, 2012).

[26] New NLRB regulations have drastically affected employee speech on social media. *See, e.g.,* Cayce Myers, *The New Water Cooler: Implications for Practitioners Concerning the NLRB's Stance on Social Media and Workers' Rights,* 40 PUB. REL. REV. 547 (2014).

applicants.[27] The law has two key provisions that forbid an employer to require an employee or job applicant to:

> (1) Disclose the username and password to the current or prospective employee's social media account; or
> (2) Add an employee, supervisor, or administrator to the list of contacts associated with the current or prospective employee's social media account.[28]

The law applies both to job applicants and employees. Employers may not terminate employees or refuse to hire applicants for exercising their rights under this law.[29] There are some limitations, however. Social media accounts created by an employee on behalf of an employer, provided to an employee by an employer, created under the instruction of an employer, or created by an employee to impersonate an employer are not protected.[30] However, employers may not access employees' personal social media accounts even if the employer obtains usernames or passwords inadvertently.[31] According to the National Conference of State Legislatures, as of 2015, 21 states have laws similar to Virginia's.[32]

---

[27] VA. CODE ANN. § 40.1-28.7:5 (1950).
[28] VA. CODE ANN. § 40.1-28.7:5 (B)(1)(2) (1950).
[29] VA. CODE ANN. § 40.1-28.7:5 (D) (1950).
[30] VA. CODE ANN. § 40.1-28.7:5 (A) (1950).
[31] VA. CODE ANN. § 40.1-28.7:5 (C) (1950).
[32] *See* State Laws About Social Media Privacy, http://www.ncsl.org/research/telecommunications-and-information-technology/state-laws-prohibiting-access-to-social-media-usernames-and-passwords.aspx (accessed Jan. 4, 2016).

Criminal Law in Cyberspace

The Internet can be a place where users can become victims very quickly. Like the physical world, the Internet is a forum where theft, intimidation, scams and stalking can take place. Virginia law has approached cyber crime both with new approaches to warrants for criminal evidence and with a new set of criminal statutes designed to protect the public from the dangerous side of cyberspace.

Warrants

The Fourth Amendment to the U.S. Constitution requires the government to obtain a warrant based on probable cause prior to searching an area where a person has a "reasonable expectation of privacy." [33] Even though search warrants require police to identify specific locations for searches, warrantless searches are legal under some circumstances. [34] However, as a general rule, any evidence obtained by an illegal or warrantless search is excluded as evidence at trial as "fruit of the poisonous tree."[35]

Virginia law mandates that searches must be conducted in a reasonable way, and a search cannot go beyond the limits of the warrant. [36] Warrants for computer searches are allowed under Virginia law, but issues arise when a computer contains files or folders that contain unrelated information. In *Rosa v.*

---

[33] Katz v. United States, 389 U.S. 347, 360 (1967).

[34] *See* Arizona v. Gant, 556 U.S. 332 (2009); Carroll v. United States, 267 U.S. 132 (1925).

[35] Nardone v. United States, 308 U.S. 338, 341 (1938).

[36] *See, e.g.,* Murphy v. Commonwealth, 427 S.E.2d 228 (Va. 1993); Kearney v. Commonwealth., 355 S.E.2d 897 (Va. Ct. App. 1987).

Commonwealth, the Virginia Court of Appeals held that an officer who used a keyword search to obtain incriminating information from a suspect's computer acted within the scope of the search warrant.[37] The court reasoned that searches can include non-relevant information and the scope of a search can contain areas around where the search is conducted.

Cyber Crime

The Virginia Code has a specific section titled the "Virginia Computer Crimes Act" that deals with crime in cyberspace.[38] Under the law, computer data, programs and software are considered property. The laws criminalize computer fraud,[39] emailed spam, online trespass, privacy invasion, illegally gathering personal information, stealing computer services, using a computer to physically harm another, harassment, and embezzlement. Penalties for violating these statutes range from misdemeanor fines, such as for computer harassment, to felony punishment, such as for personal trespass by computer.

---

[37] 628 S.E.2d 92 (Va. App. 2006).

[38] VA. CODE ANN. §§ 18.2-152.2-18.2-152.8, 18.2-152.12, 18.2-152.14 (1950).

[39] VA. CODE ANN. §18.2-152.3 (1950) (A discussion of federal preemption of this statute can be found in *SecureInfo Corp. v. Telos Corp.*, 387 F. Supp. 2d 593 (E.D. Va. 2005).); VA. CODE ANN. §18.2-152.3:1 (1950) (spam); VA. CODE ANN. §18.2-152.4 (1950) (online trespass); VA. CODE ANN. §18.2-152.5 (1950) (privacy); VA. CODE ANN. §18.2-152.5:1 (1950) (personal information); VA. CODE ANN. §18.2-152.6 (1950) (theft of computer services); VA. CODE ANN. §18.2-152.7 (1950) (physical harm); VA. CODE ANN. §18.2-152.7:1 (1950) (harassment); VA. CODE ANN. §18.2-152.8 (1950) (embezzlement); VA. CODE ANN. §18.2-152.7:1 (1950) (computer harassment); VA. CODE ANN. §18.2-152.7 (1950) (felony punishment).

While some of these statutes have not received much attention from Virginia courts, others have been fiercely debated. In 2015, the Virginia Court of Appeals held that a state trooper who ran unauthorized background checks through Virginia Criminal Information Network violated Virginia's statute against using computers for privacy invasion. The court held that the trooper acted without authority when running names of her known acquaintances.[40] In 2008, the Virginia Supreme Court held that out-of-state defendants could be tried under Virginia law banning spam emails.[41]

However, some computer statutes allow for damages in civil lawsuits arising from computer trespass.[42] These cases are less common, but there are some notable exceptions. In a Harrisonburg case, an accounting firm sought multiple types of damages under the computer privacy statute for the alleged theft of computer files by a former employee.[43] The former employee used this information to recruit the firm's employees for a new business and poach the firm's clients. Ultimately the court ruled that, although the accounting firm could recover compensatory and liquidated damages, there was no statutory right to punitive damages. [44]

---

[40] Ramsey v. Commonwealth, 780 S.E.2d 624 (Va. Ct. App. 2015).

[41] Jaynes v. Commonwealth, 666 S.E.2d 303 (Va. 2008). A more detailed discussion of this case can be found in Chapter 3.

[42] VA. CODE ANN. §18.2-152.12 (2010). *See also* VA. CODE ANN. §18.2-152.4 (1950).

[43] McGladrey & Pullen LLP v. Shrader, 62 Va. Cir. 401 (Cir. Ct. 2003) (Rockingham County).

[44] *Id.* Compensatory damages are money losses suffered by a party in a lawsuit. Liquidated damages are money losses

Similarly, in 2014, a former Virginia Commonwealth University professor sued the university alleging, among other things, that the university violated a statute which banned invasion of privacy by computer.[45] The federal court for the Eastern District of Virginia ultimately dismissed the case, holding that the university had a right to monitor the professor's computer during his employment.[46]

---

given to a party when there is a specific breach of contract. Punitive damages are money damages imposed on a defendant as a punishment and deterrent for their actions.

[45] *See* VA. CODE ANN. §18.2-152.2 (1950).

[46] Walsh v. Logothetis, No. 3:13CV401-JAG, 2014 WL 229588 (E.D. Va. Jan. 21, 2014). This case was also notable for the number of defendants sued. The plaintiff brought suit against 17 separate defendants in a 91-page complaint.

5. LIBEL

In Old Virginia, an insult could prompt fisticuffs or, worse yet, a pistol duel. Violent responses to verbal insults became so common, in fact, that, in 1810, the Virginia General Assembly adopted what has become known as "the insulting words statute," specifically to force disputes from the streets into courtrooms.[1]

The effort worked. Dueling was reduced, but battles in the courtroom, in their own way, were no easier settled than they had been in the streets. Libel cases in Virginia, like everywhere else, are difficult to resolve. Complex burdens of proof require extensive preparation and hours of complicated deposition taking and evidence presentation. Both plaintiffs and defendants face grueling tasks.

Before turning to an examination of how libel law works, however, some background on libel in Virginia is necessary.

---

[1] VA. CODE ANN. § 8.01-45 55 (1950). The Virginia Supreme Court noted in 1887 that the purpose of the statute was to suppress "the barbarous custom of dueling." Chaffin v. Lynch, 1 S.E. 803, 806 (Va. 1887). For a good brief history of libel law in Virginia, *see* David C. Kohler, *Toward a Modern Defamation Law in Virginia: Questions Answered, Questions Raised,* 21 RICH. L. REV. 3, 41-44 (1986). Also helpful in the preparation of this chapter was Alexander Wellford & Craig T. Merritt, *Survey of Virginia Defamation Law,* LIBEL DEFENSE RESOURCE CENTER 50-STATE SURVEY 1999-2000.

THE DEVELOPMENT OF LIBEL LAW IN VIRGINIA

The insulting words statute and Virginia common law have spawned lawsuits that fall into three distinct classes: insulting words, libel and slander. Early in the history of libel law, lawsuits could be filed when words were written or spoken that "from their usual construction and common acceptance are construed as insults and tend to violence and breach of the peace."[2] Depending upon the circumstances, a lawsuit might have fallen into any of the three categories. The causes of action were similar in many ways, but there were some important differences.

Libel involved written words that, like slander or insulting words, might cause a breach of the peace. The cause of action was not related to whether a person was actually injured, but was based on insult, embarrassment or hurt feelings. Since injured feelings existed regardless of whether a published charge was true or false, truth was no defense. A requirement for a successful libel action was that the insulting words be published to some third party, that is, to someone other than the author and the subject of the alleged defamation.

Similarly, since an insult involved words – spoken or written – specifically intended to harm an individual, truth was no defense in an insulting words case. Unlike libel, however, whether a third person heard or read the words was irrelevant – it was necessary only for the person at whom the words were aimed to hear them.

The third type of legal action in Virginia's defamation history was slander, which involved

---

[2] VA. CODE ANN. § 8.01-45 (1950).

spoken words that caused specific monetary loss. The sole basis for a slander suit was whether a person had suffered some pecuniary loss that could be documented. Like libel, publication to a third party was necessary for the suit to be actionable.

As Virginia's libel law evolved, the three causes of action were merged. Virginia courts no longer recognize a distinction between an action for libel and an action for slander,[3] and have established that the only distinction between an action for libel and one for insulting words is that publication to a third party is necessary for a successful libel action.[4] In fact, under modern Virginia law, an action for insulting words cannot exist absent a libel case unless the words may also be construed as fighting words.[5]

Libel, which is the focus of this chapter, may also be brought under Virginia common law.[6] Libel occurs when words are published in some written form

---

[3] *See, e.g.,* Fleming v. Moore, 275 S.E.2d 632, 635 (Va. 1981) (citing Shupe v. Roses' Stores, 192 S.E.2d 766, 767 (1972)).

[4] *See* Hines v. Gravins, 112 S.E. 869, 870 (Va. 1922); Davis v. Heflin, 107 S.E. 673, 675 (Va. 1921).

[5] *See* Dwyer v. Smith, 867 F.2d 184, 195-96 (4th Cir. 1989). Fighting words are discussed in Chapter 3. While an action for fighting words generally requires a face-to-face confrontation, under Virginia law an insulting words claim can be either spoken or in writing if there is a likelihood that the words could lead to violence. *See* Trail v. Gen. Dynamics Armament and Technical Products, Inc., 697 F. Supp. 2d 654, 658 (W.D. Va. 2010).

[6] *See Shupe*, 192 S.E.2d at 767.

that tend to injure the reputation of a person or to render that person odious, contemptible or ridiculous.[7]

Libel law is not that simple, however. Modern libel law recognizes that some forms of defamation are justified. It is defamatory, for example, to report that a mayor is accepting bribes for assuring that certain businesses receive contracts with his city. The report would certainly injure the mayor's reputation and would render him contemptible. If the report is true, however, or is published after it was thoroughly investigated, the publisher of such a report is not likely to lose a libel action.

Responsible news organizations, therefore, cannot fulfill their role in society without publishing defamations. But only unjustified defamations are punishable. The responsibility for proving that punishment is warranted lies with the plaintiff.

THE LIBEL PLAINTIFF

To win a libel action in Virginia, a plaintiff must prove that there was publication of a false, actionable statement about the plaintiff, to some third person, that tended to injure the plaintiff's reputation.[8] The plaintiff must also prove that there was some degree of fault on the part of the defendant.[9] In simplest terms, then, a libel plaintiff's burden of proof consists of six elements: publication, identification, defamation, falsity, damages and fault.

---

[7] Chaffin v. Lynch, 1 S.E. 803, 807 (Va. 1887).

[8] *Libel & Slander* §12, MICHIE'S JURISPRUDENCE OF VIRGINIA & WEST VIRGINIA (1948).

[9] *See* Gazette, Inc. v. Harris, 325 S.E.2d 713 (Va. 1985); Fleming v. Moore, 275 S.E.2d 632 (Va. 1981).

Publication

The defendant in a libel action is not necessarily the author of defamatory material; libel law is generally unconcerned with authors. The person who faces liability is the publisher – that person who makes the defamatory material available to some third party. A person may – with complete immunity – write anything about anyone. In addition, an author may show the defamatory material to the person about whom it is written without fear of liability.[10] If the author shows the material to anyone else, however, the material has been published and a lawsuit is possible.[11] The author is not being sued for creating the defamation, but for publishing it.

Publication is probably the easiest element for a libel plaintiff to prove, particularly in cases involving the media. While plaintiffs in non-media libel actions may lose their cases because they could not show that the defamatory material had been published,[12] publication is almost never at issue in cases involving

---

[10] While no libel action would be successful under the circumstances described here, at one time Virginia law would have allowed an action for insulting words. *See* discussion accompanying *supra* notes 2-5.

[11] *See, e.g.,* Davis v. Heflin, 107 S.E. 673 (Va. 1921) (The mailing of a letter to a third person is held to be publication.). An exception to the rule is sharing the allegedly defamatory material with someone who has a duty related to the incidents described in the publication. *See, e.g.,* Cobb v. Rector and Visitors of the Univ. of Virginia, 84 F. Supp. 2d 740, 750 (W.D. Va. 2000).

[12] *See, e.g.,* Dwyer v. Smith, 867 F.2d 184, 195 (4th Cir. 1989); Food Lion, Inc. v. Melton, 485 S.E.2d 580, 584-85 (Va. 1995).

mass communication. The plaintiff only needs to show that the questionable material appeared in some published form – a newspaper, magazine, book, brochure, poster, film, Web page or broadcast, for example. It is not necessary to prove that someone actually saw the allegedly defamatory material; if it appeared in a mass medium, the presumption is that it was published. This last point is particularly noteworthy in cases involving the posting of material on an Internet Web page.

Since the publisher, rather than the author, is the target of a libel action, however, newspapers and magazines can be sued for publishing material produced by non-employees: by free-lance writers, by news and feature syndicates, by advertisers and even by readers.[13]

In addition, each time a defamation is published, the republication is considered a new libel, and the publisher of the new libel may be sued. In some cases – if the republication "is the natural and probable consequence" of the original publication – the original publisher can also be sued for the republication.[14] In one 1989 Virginia case, for example, the Fourth U.S. Circuit Court of Appeals held that a publisher of financial information was responsible for a defamatory article published by the

---

[13] *See, e.g.,* Story v. Norfolk-Portsmouth Newspapers, Inc., 118 S.E.2d 668 (Va. 1961), in which the *Virginian-Pilot* was sued for material published in a letter to the editor.

[14] *See* Weaver v. Beneficial Fin. Co., 98 S.E.2d 687, 690 (Va. 1957).

Roanoke Times & World-News because the article was based on a report issued by the company.[15]

Identification

In legal parlance, "identification" means that the defamatory material is "of and concerning" the plaintiff. The plaintiff is required to prove that the defamation specifically identified him or her.[16]

Identification is usually easy to prove. When a person is named, that person has been identified. There are other methods of identification, however. Someone may be identified by use of a photograph or cartoon, for example. And, of course, identification can be based entirely upon description. That has happened in at least two Virginia cases – one from the Virginia Supreme Court and one from the federal court for the Eastern District of Virginia.[17]

Port Packet Corp. v. Lewis was one of four cases the Virginia Supreme Court resolved under the title *Gazette, Inc. v. Harris.*[18] The case involved two

---

[15] Blue Ridge Bank v. Veribanc, Inc., 866 F.2d 681, 689-90 (4th Cir. 1989).

[16] In March 2001, the Virginia Supreme Court refused to allow a law suit to proceed when the plaintiff in the case wanted to remain anonymous. America Online v. Anonymous Publicly Traded Co., 542 S.E.2d 377 (Va. 2001)

[17] Federal courts play a limited role in libel actions; they are required to rule in accordance with state law or, in the absence of precedent, to rule as they determine state courts would.

[18] 325 S.E.2d 713 (Va. 1985). In addition to the *Gazette* case, 325 S.E.2d at 728, and *Port Packet v. Lewis,* 325 S.E.2d at 735, the cases settled in the opinion were *Charlottesville Newspapers, Inc. v. Matthews*, 325 S.E.2d at 732, and *Fleming v. Moore*, 325 S.E.2d at 742. This was the second time *Fleming*

articles and an editorial on child abuse published by the *Alexandria Port Packet* in July 1980. In one article, the newspaper identified with the fictional name of "Mark" a nine-month-old boy who died in an Alexandria hospital. "Mark" died of severe head injuries two days after being admitted to the hospital. The article reported that police believed "Mark" to be the victim of "a vicious attack." "Mark's" parents were not named in the article, and a last name for the child was not used.[19]

The newspaper was sued by E. Grey Lewis and Carolyn G. Lewis, however, who argued that they had been identified as abusive parents. Though not named, they said the many similarities between "Mark" and their own son, Edward, would cause readers to believe the Lewises were responsible for their son's death.[20]

The Virginia Supreme Court agreed. Like "Mark," Edward was nine months old and had severe head injuries. Edward was admitted to the same hospital as "Mark," was in the hospital the same length of time before dying, and died at about the same time as "Mark." In addition, the court found to be significant the newspaper's stated intent to identify abusive parents. The jury could have concluded, therefore, that the newspaper intended to refer directly to "Mark's" abusers and, in so doing, had identified

---

reached the Virginia Supreme Court. *See* text accompanying *infra* notes 40-41.

[19] 325 S.E.2d at 736.

[20] *Id.* at 735-36. *See also* Pendleton v. Newsome, 772 S.E.2d 759 (Va. 2015) (A reference to "parents" was sufficient to identify the mother of a young girl who died form ingesting peanuts at her school.).

the Lewises as abusive parents.[21] This was so, the court found, even though neither the reporter who wrote the article nor his editors knew the true identities of "Mark" or his parents.[22]

In some cases, description need not be nearly so specific for a court to rule that a plaintiff was identified. A single reference to a "live-in lover" in a satirical song broadcast by a radio station was sufficient for identification in the case of *Freedlander v. Edens Broadcasting, Inc.,* out of the Eastern District of Virginia.[23]

Eric M. Freedlander and Donna Leigh Keeler sued WRVQ for broadcasting a song they said defamed them. Freedlander, a well-known Richmond businessman, was identified by name, but Keeler was not. She brought suit alleging that the station identified her by a reference to Freedlander's live-in lover. The court agreed,[24] noting that Keeler had been referred to in news articles as Freedlander's roommate and companion.[25]

Virginia law also recognizes that members of groups can be identified, even if not named, if the groups are relatively small. If a group is very large, however, individuals may not bring libel actions because the size of the group precludes the identification of individual members. It has been difficult to pinpoint the threshold that allows

---

[21] *Id.* at 738-39.

[22] *Id.* at 739.

[23] 734 F. Supp. 221 (E.D. Va. 1990).

[24] *Id.* at 224.

[25] *Id.* at 227 n.11.

identification, but it generally lies between twenty-five and one hundred.[26]

Not so in Virginia, where a group of five might be too large.

There have been only two appellate cases in which group libel was discussed. In 1924, the state supreme court ruled that a member of the House of Delegates was not identified in a publication that criticized, but did not name, one member of the general assembly. The court held:

> If the class or group is a very large one, and there is little or nothing which applies to the particular person who brings the action, his right of recovery will generally be denied. . . . On the other hand, if the language employed is directed towards a comparatively small or restricted group of persons, then any member thereof may sue.[27]

Seventy-eight years later, the same court indicated that a police department of some five to eight members was too large for one of its officers to prove identification.[28] Elkton police officer Donald A. Dean sued M. Lee Dearing because of critical comments Dearing had made about the police department, which

---

[26] A good discussion of group libel is Kyu Ho Youm, *Defamation, in* COMMUNICATION AND THE LAW 94 (W. Wat Hopkins ed. 2016).

[27] Ewell v. Boutwell, 121 S.E. 912, 914 (Va. 1924).

[28] Dean v. Dearing, 561 S.E.2d 686 (Va. 2002).

had five to eight officers at the time.[29] The court held that a member of a governmental group could sustain a libel action only by showing that the defamation was aimed specifically at the group member or at each member of the group, and Dean was unable to do so.[30]

Virginia cases related to the issue of identification are limited, but *Port Packet* and *Freedlander,* in particular, seem to indicate that courts in the commonwealth are likely to give a libel plaintiff the benefit of the doubt. If courts determine that a reasonable person might be able to identify an individual from references in a defamatory publication, the courts are likely to rule that identification has been proved. Indeed, the state supreme court has indicated that identification can occur over a series of separate publications – some of which do not identify a plaintiff. Dr. Stephen M. Levin, an orthopedist, sued WJLA-TV, a Washington, D.C., television station that broadcasts into Virginia. The station advertised an investigative report it had prepared about allegations that Levin had inappropriately treated a number of women with a technique they claimed was tantamount to sexual assault. Levin based his lawsuit on a combination of the promos, alleging that he was identified even though some of the promos did not refer to him by name, but only to "the X-rated doctor" or "the dirty doc."[31] WJLA argued that Levin was not identified in all the advertisements, but the court held:

---

[29] *Id.* at 688.

[30] *Id.* at 689.

[31] WJLA-TV v. Levin, 564 S.E.2d 383, 389-91 (Va. 2002).

> [W]e are of the opinion that statements or publications by the same defendant regarding one specific subject or event and made over a relatively short period of time, some of which clearly identify the plaintiff and others which do not, may be considered together for the purpose of establishing that the plaintiff was the person "of or concerning" whom the alleged statements were made. This is so even where the publication identifying the plaintiff is made subsequent to those that do not identify him.[32]

Defamation

Libel plaintiffs, in order to win their cases, must prove that published material tends to lower their reputations or cause them harm. The words themselves, taken in "their plain and natural meaning," must be harmful.[33] If they are, the defamation is called libel *per se* – libel on its face. Virginia also recognizes libel *per quod,* which occurs when published words are not defamatory on their face, but become defamatory when additional, unpublished facts are taken into account.[34] Special damages must also be proved in a case of libel *per quod.*

---

[32] *Id.* at 390.

[33] Carwile v. Richmond Newspapers, 82 S.E.2d 588, 591-92 (Va. 1954).

[34] A good discussion of libel *per quod* is in *Wilder v. Johnson Publishing Co.,* 551 F. Supp. 622, 623-25 (E.D. Va. 1982). *See also* Shupe v. Roses' Stores, 192 S.E.2d 766, 767 (Va. 1972).

In Virginia, published material is libelous *per se* if:[35]

(1) it charges an individual with some criminal offense involving moral turpitude for which the person could be indicted and punished;

(2) it charges an individual with having some contagious disease that would exclude the person from society;

(3) it charges an individual with being unfit to perform the duties of the person's job or with an absence of integrity needed to perform those duties;

(4) it damages a person's ability to earn a living.

Only words that fit into one of these four categories are libelous *per se* and can be the basis of a lawsuit without proof of special damages. It is not libelous *per se* in Virginia to report that someone is insane, for example, since a charge of insanity does not fall into one of the four categories, even though such a report is likely to injure a person's reputation and even though many states would recognize such a report to be defamatory. For such a charge to be actionable in Virginia, there must be a showing of special damages.[36]

Similarly, a false report that a person is dead does not fall into one of the four categories and,

---

[35] *Carwile,* 82 S.E.2d at 591. *See also* M. Rosenberg & Sons v. Craft, 29 S.E.2d 375, 378 (Va. 1944).

[36] *See M. Rosenberg,* 29 S.E.2d at 378; Mills v. Kingsport Times-News, 475 F. Supp. 1005, 1008-09 (W.D. Va. 1979).

therefore, is not libelous *per se.*[37] And, in a heated union dispute, the words "cocksucker" and "motherfucker" did not convey a false representation of any illegal acts, so they were not defamatory.[38] But a report that an attorney is unethical is likely to directly affect the attorney's profession, so the charge is libelous *per se.*[39]

The Virginia Supreme Court's strict adherence to the four categories of libel *per se* can be seen in a 1981 case involving a charge that a white professor at the University of Virginia was a racist. While racism might be an offensive charge, it is neither a contagious disease nor a criminal offense, the court held, so it was not libelous *per se.* In addition, the court originally held that there was no showing that the charge injured the professor's ability to earn a living; the fact that it "might have" affected the plaintiff's work was insufficient.[40] During the second trial of the case, however, the professor was able to introduce evidence that, on appeal, satisfied the court that a charge of racism would materially affect his relations with his students and the atmosphere in his classroom, so the charge was held to be defamatory.[41]

---

[37] *See* O'Neil v. Edmonds, 157 F. Supp. 649, 651 (E.D. Va. 1958).

[38] Crawford v. United Steel Workers, AFL-CIO, 335 S.E.2d 828, 838-39 (Va. 1985).

[39] *Carwile,* 82 S.E.2d at 592. *But see* Fuste v. Riveride Healthcare Ass'n, Inc., 578 S.E.2d 858, 860 (Va. 2003) (holding that a statement that physicians might be unprofessional or unethical was a statement of opinion.)

[40] Fleming v. Moore*,* 275 S.E.2d 632, 636 (Va. 1981).

[41] Gazette v. Harris, 325 S.E.2d 713, 744 (Va. 1985).

Despite the apparently clear language used to specify the types of words that are defamatory *per se,* some definitional problems have arisen. The first of the four categories, for example, seems to imply that virtually any charge that a person has committed a criminal offense is defamatory. The Virginia Supreme Court, however, has apparently adopted the rule that for such a charge to be actionable, the crime must be serious – a felony, "punishable by imprisonment in a state or federal institution" – or it must be "regarded by public opinion as involving moral turpitude."[42] A defamation action may be maintained, however, "[E]ven when the plaintiff actually has been charged with the offense, entered a plea of no contest, and is convicted and sentenced for the crime."[43] The ruling came in a case in which a police officer made a number of disparaging remarks about the accused. Despite the fact that the accused was convicted, he was still able to sue the officer.[44]

Charges that a person is guilty of a misdemeanor, however, are not actionable unless the misdemeanor involves moral turpitude, which the court defined as, "'[A]n act of baseness, vileness, or depravity in the private and social duties which a man owes to his fellow man, or to society in general, contrary to the accepted and customary rule of right

---

[42] Great Coastal Express, Inc. v. Ellington, 334 S.E.2d 846, 850 (Va. 1985).

[43] Lewis v. Kei, 708 S.E.2d 884, 892 (Va. 2011).

[44] *Id.*

and duty between man and man.'"[45] Under that construction, the court held that a charge of "commercial bribery" in business, while not punishable by imprisonment, was an offense involving moral turpitude and, as such, was defamatory *per se.*[46]

The state supreme court, during the same year, found that identifying a woman as being unmarried and pregnant resulted in a charge that the woman had committed the crime of fornication and was defamatory *per se. Charlottesville Newspapers, Inc. v. Matthews* was one of the four cases the court resolved in its *Gazette* opinion. Debra C. Matthews, who was married and pregnant, brought suit because she was repeatedly identified in a news story as "Miss Matthews." She was a key witness in the trial of a man she said raped her. The man was found not guilty of rape but guilty of fornication, which is the voluntary sexual intercourse by an unmarried person and is a misdemeanor in Virginia.[47]

The court held that someone reading the story could have believed that "Miss" Matthews was also guilty of fornication and became pregnant as a result.[48] What the court failed to recognize, apparently, was that, had the newspaper reported the courtesy title

---

[45] *Id.* (quoting Tasker v. Commonwealth, 121 S.E.2d 459, 463 (Va. 1961)). *See also* Schaecher v. Bouffault, 722 S.E.2d 589, 595 (Va. 2015) (holding that even if the owner of a kennel violated easements, covenants or ordinances in seeking to expand the kennel, those violations did not amount to what the court called "reprehensible crimes").

[46] *Id.*

[47] Gazette v. Harris, 325 S.E.2d 713, 732-33 (Va. 1985).

[48] *Id.* at 733.

correctly, the reader could have presumed that Mrs. Matthews may have been guilty of adultery, which would have been no less defamatory.[49]

Ironically, a federal district court in Virginia ruled five years later that the crime of fornication did not involve moral turpitude, within the definition adopted by the Virginia Supreme Court, and, therefore, was not defamatory.[50] In *Freedlander v. Edens Broadcsting, Inc.,* which involved a woman who was identified as a "live-in lover," the court ruled that cohabitation and fornication might have once involved moral turpitude, but no longer. "This is evidenced," the court held, "by the absence of prosecutorial vigor." There have been no arrests for such behavior, the court noted, and the crimes were established to inhibit prostitution.[51]

In addition, in the same case, the court held that it is not defamatory *per se* to report that someone is in bankruptcy and is subject to criminal investigation, because neither of these charges suggests the commission of an offense punishable by imprisonment.[52]

Indeed, it has been difficult for courts to settle on exactly what a crime involving moral turpitude is. Lying on legal documents, for example, is a crime

---

[49] *See* Kohler, *supra* note 1, at 29.

[50] Freedlander v. Edens Broad., 734 F. Supp. 221, 226 (E.D. Va. 1990). *See* discussion of this case accompanying *supra* notes 23-25.

[51] *Id.*

[52] *Id.* at 225.

involving moral turpitude,[53] but concealing liquor on which taxes have not been paid,[54] operating a lottery and gambling house,[55] and drunkenness[56] are not crimes involving moral turpitude.

Other examples of defamatory statements are:

- that a jewelry salesman is a shark,[57] or that a salesman is inefficient and provides unsatisfactory service;[58]
- a charge of shoplifting;[59]
- a charge that a corporation or its personnel pose a serious security risk;[60]
- a charge that a black politician's failure to support a second black politician harmed the black community.[61]
- that a person is a "thug" and "gangster."[62]

---

[53] Chesapeake and Ohio Ry. Co. v. Hanes, 86 S.E.2d 122, 126 (Va. 1955).

[54] Burford v. Commonwealth, 20 S.E.2d 509, 514 (Va. 1942).

[55] Parr v. Commonwealth, 96 S.E.2d 160, 164 (Va. 1957).

[56] Pike v. Eubank, 90 S.E.2d 821, 827 (Va. 1956).

[57] Powell v. Young, 144 S.E. 624, 626 (Va. 1928).

[58] Montgomery Ward v. Nance, 182 S.E. 264, 269 (Va. 1935), *but see* discussion accompanying *infra* note 65.

[59] Zayre of Virginia, Inc. v. Gowdy, 147 S.E.2d 710, 713 (Va. 1966); Food Lion, Inc. v. Melton, 485 S.E.2d 580, 585 (Va. 1995).

[60] Swengler v. ITT Corp. Electro-Optical Products Div., 993 F.2d 1063, 1071 (4th Cir. 1993).

[61] Wilder v. Johnson Publ'g Co., 551 F. Supp. 622, 625 (E.D. Va. 1982).

Some examples of non-defamatory statements are:

- a charge that someone is discourteous;[63]
- a statement that checks should not be accepted from an individual;[64]
- a statement that an individual was terminated from his position because his job performance was unsatisfactory.[65]

Virginia law specifies that, for words to be considered defamatory, they "are to be taken in their natural sense, and as they would naturally be understood by those reading [the] publication."[66] This does not mean, however, that the defamation must always be explicit. As the state supreme court has held:

> [I]t is not necessary that the defamatory charge be in direct terms but it may be made indirectly, and it matters not how artful or disguised the modes in which the meaning is concealed if it is in fact defamatory.

---

[62] Choi v. Kyu Chul Lee, 312 Fed.Appx. 551, 533 (4th Cir. 2009).

[63] Auvil v. Times-Journal Co., 10 Media L. Rep. (BNA) 2302, 2303 (E.D. Va. 1984).

[64] Shupe v. Rose's Stores, 192 S.E.2d 766. 767 (Va. 1972).

[65] McBride v. City of Roanoke Redevelopment and Housing Auth., 871 F. Supp. 885, 891-92 (W.D. Va. 1994), *but see* discussion accompanying *supra* note 58.

[66] Ewell v. Boutwell, 121 S.E. 912, 916 (Va. 1924).

> Accordingly, a defamatory charge may be made by inference, implication or insinuation.[67]

But, the court added, "[T]he meaning of the alleged defamatory language cannot, by innuendo, be extended beyond its ordinary and common acceptation."[68] Questions therefore, are not defamatory if the context of those questions indicates that several answers exist, since inquiry, however embarrassing or unpleasant to its subject, is not defamatory. If the questions, however, may be read as assertions of fact, they may be defamatory. The language must be read so as to "make that certain which is in fact uncertain."[69]

A 2014 Virginia Supreme Court case demonstrates the difficulty in demonstrating defamation by innuendo. The *Virginian-Pilot* reported that a student who received no discipline for his role in a physical confrontation at school was the son of an assistant principal at a different school. The administrator sued the newspaper for the accurate report of the incident, but alleged that the newspaper had implied that he had an impact on how his son was treated. The question, the court held, was whether "the article is reasonably capable of the defamatory

---

[67] Carwile v. Richmond Newspapers, 82 S.E.2d 588, 592 (Va. 1954). *See also* Zayre of Virginia, Inc. v. Gowdy, 147 S.E.2d 710, 713 (Va. 1966).

[68] *Id.*

[69] Chapin v. Knight-Ridder, Inc., 993 F.2d 1087, 1094 (4th Cir. 1993).

meaning . . . ascribe[d] to it."[70] While the article might have suggested that the assistant principal had "an uncommon acquaintance with administrators at his son's school" and that relationship might have played a role in the way his son was treated, the article was not reasonably capable of defamatory meaning.[71]

Falsity

Falsity is a key element in a libel action, since only false statements are actionable. To publish that the mayor accepts bribes, as previously indicated, will certainly damage the mayor's reputation, but a news organization cannot be required to pay damages for publishing the statement if it is true. Similarly, a commentator cannot be required to pay damages for stating the opinion that the mayor has done a poor job while in office. Since opinions are neither true nor false, in Virginia they are not actionable. Opinion is discussed in detail later in this chapter.

The Virginia Supreme Court has held that a plaintiff in a libel action is required to prove that the published, defamatory material is false.[72] That is, the court made a clear distinction between defamation and falsity. Words may be defamatory, the court held, but unless those same words are false, there can be no libel action.[73] In addition, the material shown to be false must be at the heart of the libel claim. It is insufficient

---

[70] Webb v. Virginian-Pilot Media Corp., 752 S.E.2d 808, 811 (Va. 2014).

[71] *Id.* at 812.

[72] Gazette v. Harris, 325 S.E.2d 713, 724-25 (Va. 1985).

[73] Shenandoah Publ'g House, Inc. v. Gunter, 427 S.E.2d 370, 372 (Va. 1993).

for the plaintiff to prove that there were some slight inaccuracies in a long publication since "slight inaccuracies of expression are immaterial."[74] Similarly, a federal court held in a Virginia case that "a plaintiff cannot combine the damaging nature of certain true statements with the falsity of other, immaterial statements in order to provide the basis for a defamation claim."[75] In addition, the issue turns on the truth of what was published. For example, the truth of a published report about a person being arrested and charged with a crime focuses on whether the individual was, in fact, arrested and charged, not on the individual's ultimate guilt or innocence.[76]

Finally, language that is merely rhetorical hyperbole, the Virginia Supreme Court has held, cannot be proved to be false and, therefore, cannot be the basis of a libel action. Attorneys for Sharon Yeagle, an administrator at Virginia Tech, argued to the court in 1998 that a line published in the *Collegiate Times,* the university's student newspaper, identifying her as "Director of Butt Licking," charged Yeagle with the crime of sodomy. The identification line was part of a computer template used in layout that editors failed to change during the production of the paper.[77]

---

[74] Saleeby v. Free Press, Inc., 91 S.E.2d 405, 407 (Va. 1956). *See also,* James v. Haymes, 178 S.E. 18, 22 (Va. 1935).

[75] Chapin v. Greve, 787 F. Supp. 557, 563 (E.D. Va. 1992).

[76] *See* Pilkenton v. Kingsport Publ'g Corp., 270 F. Supp. 315, 317 (W.D. Va. 1967), *aff'd* 395 F.2d 989 (4th Cir. 1968).

[77] Yeagle v. Collegiate Times, 497 S.E.2d 136, 137 (Va. 1998).

Montgomery Circuit Court Judge Ray Grubb dismissed the lawsuit, finding that the phrase was "void of any literal meaning" and that no reasonable person would have believed the line to convey any factual information about Yeagle.[78] The state supreme court affirmed, holding that "speech which does not contain a provably false factual connotation, or statements which cannot reasonably be interpreted as stating actual facts about a person cannot form the basis of a common law defamation action."[79] The court noted that the identification line is "disgusting, offensive and in extremely bad taste," but, "[I]t cannot reasonably be understood as stating an actual fact about Yeagle's job title or her conduct, or that she committed a crime of moral turpitude."[80]

Damages

Without proof that a defamatory publication caused actual injury, a plaintiff cannot win a defamation action. That is, the plaintiff must produce evidence that tends to prove actual injury.[81] The type of injury a plaintiff suffers is represented by three types of damages, the award of each being determined by a jury:

- *Actual* or *compensatory damages* are damages paid to a plaintiff for injury caused by libel *per se*. The damages are to compensate for an injured

---

[78] *Id.*

[79] *Id.*

[80] *Id.* at 138.

[81] *See* Isle of Wight County v. Norgiec, 704 S.E.2d 83, 87 (Va. 2011); Landmark Commc'ns, Inc. v. Macione, 334 S.E.2d 587 (Va. 1988).

reputation and the accompanying embarrassment, humiliation, emotional suffering and physical suffering. Evidence must generally be introduced demonstrating the injury. That evidence can be testimony about the negative effects the publication had on the subject of the publication. The testimony may demonstrate a personality change in the subject that the subject felt humiliation and embarrassment or that the subject feared that the attitude of neighbors and friends might change.[82] If the lawsuit is brought against a non-media defendant, is based on libel *per se,* and the material is not of public concern, however, compensatory damages are presumed if the plaintiff can demonstrate the existence of negligence.[83] Negligence is discussed in detail later in this chapter.

- *Special damages* are those for which the libel plaintiff can show specific pecuniary loss.[84] They represent out-of-pocket loss and must be documented. In cases of libel *per se,* special

---

[82] *See, e.g.,* Richmond Newspapers, Inc. v. Lipscomb, 362 S.E.2d 32, 45 (Va. 1987); Gazette v. Harris, 325 S.E.2d 713, 731, 740-41, 744-45 (Va. 1985).

[83] Great Coastal Express, Inc. v. Ellington, 334 S.E.2d 846, 852 (Va. 1985). The ruling was based in large part on the holding by the U.S. Supreme Court in *Dun & Bradstreet v Greenmoss, Inc.,* 472 U.S. 749 (1985), indicating that there is less constitutional value for words involving no matters of pubic concern. *See also* discussion accompanying *infra* notes 88-90.

[84] The Virginia Supreme Court has caused some confusion over how special damages are to be defined and awarded, but the distinction between compensatory and special damages delineated here seems to be holding true, at least for the present. *See* Kohler, *supra* note 1, at 40-41.

damages may be paid in addition to compensatory damages. In other defamation actions, a showing of special damages is required for any award.

- *Punitive damages* are awarded a plaintiff specifically to punish the publisher of a defamation for particularly reprehensible conduct. Punitive damages may not be awarded without proof of actual malice on the part of the publisher, regardless of whether the published material is of public concern.[85] Actual malice is discussed in detail later in this chapter. In Virginia, the award of punitive damages has been limited to $350,000.[86] On the surface, the limitation seems significant. Traditionally, punitive damages are considerably higher than compensatory or special damages, so a limitation on punitive damages adds a degree of protection for the press. Attorneys can always find ways to circumvent the letter of the law, however. When Tony Morrison, a former student and football player at Virginia Tech, sued the *Collegiate Times* for defamation, for example, he sought only $350,000 in punitive damages, but $5 million in compensatory damages and an additional $5 million in special damages, even though he was a student at the time and could apparently demonstrate no actual loss of income.[87]

---

[85] *See Great Coastal Express,* 334 S.E.2d at 852.

[86] VA. CODE ANN. § 8.01-38.1 (1950).

[87] Morrison v. Collegiate Times, No. 760 CL 96 B02902-00 (Cir. Ct. Richmond Co., Filed Nov. 27, 1996). Morrison eventually dropped the suit.

A libel plaintiff is required to present evidence in order to win compensatory, special or punitive damages. A type of hybrid damages – called "presumed damages" – is a holdover from the day when evidence of actual injury was not required to sustain a libel action. Presumed damages were once awarded without proof of actual injury, if a defendant was shown to have published defamatory information – the injury was presumed to have occurred because of the defamatory publication. Indeed, the Virginia Supreme Court has called such damages "presumed compensatory damages."[88] The court has also held that presumed damages may be awarded only in specific circumstances: "[W]here a private individual alleges defamation by a news-media defendant involving a matter of public concern, presumed damages cannot be awarded in the absence of actual malice."[89] Therefore, if a libel plaintiff who is a private person involved in matters of public concern convinces a jury that a media entity published a defamatory falsehood with actual

---

[88] *Great Coastal Express,* 334 S.E.2d, at 851. The court held:

> Accordingly, we hold that in an action brought by a private individual for defamatory words involving no matters of public concern, if the published words are determined by the trial judge to be actionable per se at common law, compensatory damages for injury to reputation, humiliation, and embarrassment are resumed.

Id. at 852.

[89] WJLA-TV v. Levin, 564 S.E.2d 383, 391-92 (Va. 2002). *See also, Great Coastal Express,* 334 S.E.2d at 852; Shenandoah Publ'g House, Inc. v. Gunter, 427 S.E.2d at 372.

malice, the plaintiff is not required to present evidence of damages in order to recover.[90]

Fault

The U.S. Supreme Court held in 1974 that a defamatory publication must be made with some degree of culpability on the part of the publisher before damages can be awarded.[91] The ruling, in theory, established a wide gamut of the types of fault libel plaintiffs could be required to prove in order to win their cases.

In Virginia, as in most states, however, only two types of fault have been established. Public officials and public figures are required to prove actual malice before they can win their libel actions. Private persons, on the other hand, need only prove negligence in order to win compensatory damages, but, as previously indicated, must prove actual malice if they are to win punitive damages.

Several terms, therefore, need definition: public official, public figure, actual malice and negligence.

Public officials. In *Richmond Newspapers, Inc. v. Lipscomb,*[92] the Virginia Supreme Court outlined the criteria it will use to determine whether a person is a public official. Vernelle M. Lipscomb, the head of the English Department at Thomas Jefferson High School in Richmond, sued the *Richmond Times-*

---

[90] Askew v. Collins, 722 S.E.2d 249, 251 (Va. 2012).

[91] Gertz v. Robert Welch, Inc., 418 U.S. 323, 347-48 (1974).

[92] 362 S.E.2d 32 (Va. 1987).

Dispatch for an article about students and their parents who were dissatisfied with her teaching and classroom organization. The court noted that some state courts had ruled that public school teachers were public officials,[93] but found Lipscomb to be a private person. In so doing, the court indicated five considerations that need to be addressed in determining whether a plaintiff is a public official:[94]

(1) Is the plaintiff paid with public funds? Lipscomb, as a public school teacher, was paid with public funds, but the court said other criteria were more significant.

(2) Did the plaintiff have ready access to effective means of communication? The court found that Lipscomb had limited access to the media and would have difficulty, therefore, publicly rebutting the published false statements.

(3) Is the plaintiff elected to office? Lipscomb was not.

(4) Is the plaintiff in a policy-making position? The court found that Lipscomb did not influence or appear to influence any public affairs or school policy.

(5) Is there an independent interest in the person who holds the plaintiff's position? The court found that the public had no independent interest in Lipscomb's qualifications and performance beyond a general interest in the qualifications and performance of all teachers.

---

[93] *Id.* at 36 n.3.

[94] *Id.* at 35-37.

In a case three years earlier, the federal court for the Eastern District of Virginia held that a receptionist in an Army pediatrics center was a public official.[95] The receptionist, the court held, was the single person empowered to make appointments for the clinic. In addition, her position required her to be "in constant contact with the public, including many persons who have reason to be fearful and distressed." Her performance in her position, therefore, "is clearly a matter of public concern, and accordingly, she should be treated as a public official."[96]

While it is difficult to guess what types of people may be classified as public officials by courts in Virginia, one can presume that any person elected to office will be so classified, as will almost any person in government whose position invites public scrutiny.

Public figures are equally tricky to classify.

Public Figures. Three types of public figures have been identified in Virginia cases: public figures for all purposes, also called general purpose public figures; public figures for limited purposes, or vortex public figures; and involuntary public figures. The most common, by far, are all-purpose and limited-purpose public figures.

An all-purpose public figure is a person who occupies a position of persuasive power and influence[97] or who has widespread fame or notoriety.[98]

---

[95] Auvil v. Times-Journal Co., 10 Media L. Rep. (BNA) 2302, 2304 (E.D. Va. 1984).

[96] *Id.*

[97] Fleming v. Moore, 275 S.E.2d 632, 637 (Va. 1981).

Achievement of general-purpose public-figure status is a significant feat. Neither community involvement nor newsworthiness is synonymous with public figure status. As one federal court held in a Virginia case, "The attainment of general public figure status is not to be lightly assumed, even if the plaintiff is involved in community affairs, and requires clear evidence of such stature."[99]

A limited-purpose public figure need not have achieved the widespread fame of an all-purpose public figure. Indeed, a person must meet specific requirements in order to become a public figure for limited purposes. Generally, those requirements are that:[100]

(1) there be an ongoing public controversy;

(2) the person voluntarily entered the controversy; and

(3) the person attempted to affect the outcome of the controversy.

Some courts, including the Fourth U.S. Circuit Court of Appeals in a Virginia case, have added two requirements:[101]

(4) the person has access to channels of effective communication; and

---

[98] Freedlander v. Edens Broad. Co., 734 F. Supp. 221, 229 (E.D. Va. 1990) (citing Gertz v. Robert Welch, inc., 418 U.S. 323, 351 (1974)).

[99] Blue Ridge Bank v. Veribanc, Inc., 866 F.2d 681, 687 (4th Cir. 1989).

[100] *Gertz,* 418 U.S. at 351.

[101] Fitzgerald v. Penthouse Int'l, Ltd., 691 F.2d 666, 668 (4th Cir. 1982).

(5) the person's public figure status was retained at the time of the defamation.

Because of the limited role of federal courts in state libel law, for the ruling of the Fourth U.S. Circuit Court of Appeals to be incorporated into state law, it must be adopted by the state supreme court.[102]

The same court has also broadly interpreted the requirement that there be an ongoing public controversy, holding that the controversy could be caused by the plaintiff. In *National Foundation for Cancer Research, Inc. v. Council for Better Business Bureaus, Inc.*, the court held that "[e]ven though the 'public controversy' which formed the basis of this lawsuit arose almost entirely from the Foundation's solicitation and use of funds for its cancer research, the mere fact that the NFCR generated the controversy does not preclude a finding that there was, in fact, a controversy."[103] The rationale for this broad interpretation of the rule is that a person who voluntarily engages in a course of action that invites attention and comment is a public figure.[104]

The foundation, the court held, "[V]igorously sought the public's attention" with a massive solicitation effort of almost 68 million pieces of mail over three years, in which it declared its objective to make its name a household word and "extolled its judicious use of donated funds."[105] Therefore, it

---

[102] *See supra* note 17.

[103] 705 F.2d 98, 101 (4th Cir. 1983). *See also Freedlander,* 734 F. Supp. at 230.

[104] *See Freedlander,* 734 F. Supp. at 230.

[105] *Nat'l Found.,* 705 F.2d at 101.

invited comment over its use of funds, creating a controversy, particularly since the campaign led to many inquiries of Better Business Bureaus about the foundation.[106]

Similarly, the Fourth Circuit found a scientist involved in a controversy over carcinogens to be a public figure. Melvin Reuber was employed at the Frederick Cancer Research Center, which held a contract with the National Cancer Institute. Reuber disagreed with the center on whether certain pesticides were carcinogens and reported his independent research on stationary from both the center and the institute. When he was reprimanded for his activity, a report of the reprimand was leaked to an industry newspaper. Reuber sued for libel and argued that he was a private person.[107]

The court held that (a) Reuber had significant access to channels of effective communication; (b) he voluntarily assumed a role of special prominence, (c) in order to affect the outcome of the controversy; (d) that the controversy existed prior to the publication of the defamatory statements; and, (e) that Reuber retained public figure status at the time of the publication.[108] The case was from a federal court in Maryland, but the Fourth Circuit Court would likely apply the same test to libel cases from other states within its jurisdiction.

---

[106] *Id.*

[107] Reuber v. Food Chemical News, Inc., 925 F.2d 703, 706-07 (4th Cir. 1991)(en banc).

[108] *Id.* at 708-10.

In other Virginia cases, a bank was held to be neither a public figure for general purposes nor for limited purposes because it had "no widespread power or persuasive influence" and because the controversy into which it was drawn was not of the bank's making;[109] a company hired by a county water authority was held to be neither a general-purpose nor limited-purpose public figure;[110] a chimney manufacturer whose product was disparaged in a magazine article was held to be a private person;[111] and a college professor was held to be a private person.[112]

The college professor was determined to be a private person even though he became involved in a controversy surrounding a proposed housing project near his home and spoke in opposition to the project at public hearings.[113] Similarly, the grandparents of a child involved in a prolonged and highly publicized child custody dispute, who were referred to as "abusers" and who held regular press conferences, were determined to be private persons because they did

---

[109] Blue Ridge Bank v. Veribanc, Inc., 866 F.2d 681, 687-88 (4th Cir. 1989).

[110] Arctic Co. v. Loudoun Times-Mirror, 624 F.2d 518, 521 (4th Cir. 1980).

[111] Gen. Products Co. v. Meredith Corp., 526 F. Supp. 546, 551-52 (E.D. Va. 1981).

[112] Fleming v. Moore, 275 S.E.2d 632, 637 (Va. 1991).

[113] *Id.*

not voluntarily assume a role of especial prominence.[114]

While the most common public figures are all-purpose or limited-purpose, the U.S. Supreme Court, in *Gertz,* indicated that there might be a third category of public figures: involuntary public figures. The Court noted, however, that such public figures would be "exceedingly rare."[115] And, indeed, they have been. Involuntary public figures have been discussed in only one case from Virginia. The Fourth U.S. Circuit Court of Appeals, in a 1999 case involving controversial Watergate figure G. Gordon Liddy, established a test for determining when a libel plaintiff is an involuntary public figure, but held that the person who brought a libel action against Liddy was a private person.[116] For a libel plaintiff to be an involuntary public figure, the court held, the defendant must show that:[117]

- the plaintiff had become a central figure in a significant public controversy, that the allegedly defamatory statement had arisen in the course of discussion about the public matter, and that the plaintiff was the regular focus of media reports;
- the plaintiff assumed the risk of publicity, even if not seeking to publicize views on the controversy; that is, that the plaintiff took some action or failed

---

[114] Foretich v. Capital Cities/ABC, Inc., 37 F.3d 1541, 1543 (4th Cir. 1994).

[115] Gertz v. Robert Welch, Inc., 418 U.S. 323, 345 (1974). *But see,* W. Wat Hopkins, *The Involuntary Public Figure: Not so Dead After All,* 21 CARDOZO ARTS & ENT. L.J. 1 (2003).

[116] Wells v. Liddy, 186 F.3d 505 (4th Cir. 1999).

[117] *Id.* at 539-40.

to act when action was required in circumstances in which a reasonable person would understand that publicity would likely inhere;
- the controversy existed prior to the publication of the defamatory statement;
- the plaintiff retained public figure status at the time of the defamation.

The court held that Ida Maxwell Wells, a secretary for the Democratic National Committee during the time of the Watergate break-in, was not an involuntary public figure. In a speech he gave at James Madison University, Liddy hypothesized that one reason for the break-in might have been to uncover information linking the finance of White House counsel John Dean to a supposed prostitution ring in which Wells was involved.[118] Wells was not a central figure in media reports on Watergate, the court held. Even in books promoting the call-girl theory, the court noted, Wells was not mentioned as a prominent player.[119]

Negligence and Actual Malice. As previously indicated, public officials and public figures – both limited-purpose and general-purpose – must prove actual malice in order to win their libel actions. Actual malice was defined by the U.S. Supreme Court as knowledge of falsity or reckless disregard for the truth.[120] It is a substantial burden of proof, requiring libel plaintiffs to prove either that the defendant was

---

118 *Id.* at 512.

119 *Id.* at 540-41.

120 New York Times Co. v. Sullivan, 376 U.S. 254, 279-80 (1964).

lying when he or she published the defamatory material, or that the defendant was so patently reckless that the defendant obviously did not care whether the published material was true or false.[121]

Negligence has been defined in a variety of ways,[122] and the Virginia Supreme Court has not been clear in how it defines the term. In general, the state court has defined negligence in non-libel cases as "that degree of care which an ordinarily prudent person would exercise under the same or similar circumstances to avoid injury to another."[123]

The definition is common to a number of states, but some states have interpreted negligence more broadly in media cases, indicating that an ordinarily prudent person under the same or similar circumstances would necessarily be a journalist confronted with similar problems. The definition of negligence in those states, therefore, is related to the degree of care that an ordinarily prudent journalist

---

[121] *See, e.g.,* W. WAT HOPKINS, ACTUAL MALICE 115-152 (1989). While some courts have seemed to indicate that the reckless disregard and knowledge of falsity standards of the actual malice rule run together or are a single test, it's clear the two prongs are distinctive, that is, that there are two types of actual malice: reckless disregard for the truth and knowledge of falsity. *See* Gov't Micro Resources, Inc. v. Jackson 624 S.E.2d 68, 70 (Va. 2006).

[122] *See, e.g.,* W. WAT HOPKINS, *Negligence Ten Years After Gertz v. Welch,* JOURNALISM MONOGRAPHS 5-16 (No. 93, Aug. 1985).

[123] Griffin v. Shively, 315 S.E.2d 210, 212-13 (Va. 1984) (quoting Perlin v. Chappell, 96 S.E.2d 805, 808 (Va. 1957)).

would exercise in similar circumstances.[124] This is an important distinction since actions by a reasonably prudent journalist and a reasonably prudent person may not be identical.

The Virginia Supreme Court has made several references to the "reasonably prudent" editor or journalist.[125] Indeed, in *Richmond Newspapers, Inc. v. Lipscomb,* the court specifically referred to the type of action that would be taken by "a reasonably prudent news reporter."[126]

At the same time, however, the court has demonstrated a lack of understanding of the unique character of the newsroom. In a number of cases from other states, expert witnesses have been called to testify as to actions by journalists that might or might not be reasonable. Though not ruling outright that expert witnesses would not be allowed in Virginia courts, the state supreme court – again in *Richmond Newspapers* – upheld a ruling by a trial judge denying a defendant in a libel case the right to call expert witnesses.[127] Expert witnesses are not needed, the court held, "concerning matters of common knowledge or matters as to which the jury are [sic] as competent to form an opinion as the witnesses."[128] The court did not explain how members of a jury would be knowledgeable about the operation of a newsroom or the duties and expectations of reporters.

---

[124] *See, e.g.,* HOPKINS, *supra* note 122, at 8-13.

[125] *See, e.g.,* Gazette v. Harris, 325 S.E.2d 713, 729, 733 (Va. 1985).

[126] 362 S.E.2d 32, 38 (Va. 1987).

[127] *Id.*

[128] *Id.* at 42.

Whatever the definition of negligence in Virginia, the court has established that the rule will only apply when the material in question "makes substantial danger to reputation apparent."[129] When the material is not obviously defamatory, actual malice must be proved in order to recover damages. Therefore, the court held, "The mere negligent error or careless misstatement of fact which, on its face, does not appear to be defamatory will not result in liability."[130]

On its face, the rule seems to be an added bit of protection for the press. It does not always operate that way, however, because of the way the court has applied negligence. Indeed, one attorney knowledgeable about libel law has said the application of negligence in Virginia is likely to be highly unpredictable because of the lack of precision given the term by the court.[131]

Possibly the best way to demonstrate negligence and actual malice is to examine Virginia cases in which these fault elements were delineated.[132]

---

[129] *Gazette,* 325 S.E.2d at 725.

[130] *Id.* at 725-26.

[131] Kohler, *supra* note 1, at 28.

[132] The Virginia Supreme Court has held that negligence is subsumed by actual malice. That is, if a libel plaintiff proves that a defendant published defamatory material with knowledge of falsity or reckless disregard for the truth, the plaintiff has automatically proven publication with negligence. *See* Shenandoah Publ'g House, Inc. v. Gunter, 427 S.E.2d 370, 372 (Va. 1993); Great Coastal Express, Inc. v. Ellington, 334 S.E.2d 846, 853 (Va. 1985). The ruling is only important in procedural issues, however. That is, failure to instruct a jury as to negligence

The court's first examination of negligence came in the 1985 case of *Gazette, Inc. v. Harris.* As previously indicated, the case involved four libel suits combined by the court and settled under one title. In three of the cases, the court found evidence of negligence, and in one case the court found evidence of actual malice.

The court's most detailed examination of negligence came in the first of the four cases. A Goochland County paper, the *Gazette,* had published, as part of its regular roundup of criminal court activity, the following item:

> Harold F. Payne, aggravated sexual battery, Barbara H. Sweeny, property bond; aggravated sexual battery, James and Virginia Harris, property bond charges certified to circuit court (charges filed in the adult division of juvenile court).[133]

In fact, Payne had been charged with two counts of aggravated sexual battery; Sweeny and the Harrises were the complainants, that is, they were bringing the charges against Payne. They filed suit against the *Gazette,* claiming that the item identified them as having been charged with the crimes.

An editor at the *Gazette* testified that he believed the item to be accurate because it was a verbatim copy of a court record. To complicate

---

is not reversible error if there is a finding of actual malice. *See Great Coastal,* 334 S.E.2d at 372.

[133] 325 S.E.2d at 728.

matters, until the report was published, the *Gazette* had not been in the practice of including in its "Criminal Cases" column the names of complainants; previously only the persons charged had been named. The newspaper's failure to explain the significance of the names, the court held, was carelessness.[134] A jury could reasonably find, therefore, that the newspaper acted negligently in violating its long-standing custom of only publishing the names of suspects without using a format that accurately informed readers of the significance of the names.[135]

But this was only part of the evidence of negligence. In affirming verdicts for Sweeny and the Harrises, the Virginia Supreme Court also found it significant that neither the reporter nor his editor sought verification for the information. That was important, the court said, because the reporter did not fully understand the documents he was examining: "The jury was entitled to conclude that the reporter was negligent because of his ignorance."[136]

In addition, evidence indicated that the only part of the court document the reporter understood was the abbreviation "CMPLNT," for "complainant." Yet, the reporter failed to identify Sweeny and the Harrises as the complainants, "an act of omission that the jury also could determine constituted negligence."[137]

In neither of the other two *Gazette* opinion cases involving negligence was the court so exacting in

---

[134] *Id.* at 730.

[135] *Id.* at 731.

[136] *Id.* at 730.

[137] *Id.*

its examination of the facts. In *Charlottesville Newspapers, Inc. v. Matthews,* which has been discussed previously, the court found *The Daily Progress* negligent when it identified a married woman as pregnant and unmarried.

Once again, the report was written by a reporter who was inexperienced in covering courts. He based his report on a transcript of a preliminary hearing in the case, rather than attending the trial or using a transcript of the trial, and he did not talk to anyone involved in the case. In addition, he testified that the use of "Miss" rather than "Mrs." to identify the plaintiff was, "Just a slip of my memory," and the city editor testified that it never occurred to him that calling a woman "Miss" and identifying her as pregnant would be defamatory. Because of all this, the court held, "[E]vidence of the newspaper's negligence was abundant."[138]

The final negligence case in the *Gazette* opinion has also been discussed previously. E. Gray and Carolyn G. Lewis sued the *Alexandria Port Packet* claiming they were identified as abusive parents because circumstances surrounding the death of an unidentified child in an article published by the newspaper were similar to those of their own child. The article quoted Alexandria Police Sergeant Ronald Uhrig as saying the child died as a result of a vicious attack, that the child was the victim of a beating and that the police were treating the child's death as a murder. At trial, however, Uhrig testified that he never

---

[138] *Id.* at 734. *See* discussion of the case at *supra* notes 45-47.

made those comments and that he had complained to the reporter about being misquoted.[139]

In addition, the reporter sought no verification of the information he received for the story because he mistakenly believed Uhrig to be in charge of the investigation into
the child's death.[140]

While this was evidence of negligence, the court held, there was no evidence of actual malice; there was no evidence that the reporter or his editor knew the defamatory material was false, and, "[T]he articles were researched in depth" and were "edited in a deliberate fashion with consideration given to accuracy."[141]

Research also became an issue in determining the existence of negligence and actual malice two years later when the court decided *Richmond Newspapers, Inc. v. Lipscomb.*[142] Vernelle Lipscomb was a high school English teacher who was harshly criticized by some of her students and their parents in an article written by *Richmond Times-Dispatch* reporter Charles E. Cox. The article was initiated when a parent contacted Cox about problems students were having with Lipscomb. The reporter wrote the story after talking with at least three parents, at least three students, several of Lipscomb's colleagues, Lipscomb's principal and other administrators.

---

139 *Id.* at 736-37. *See* discussion of the case at *supra* notes 18-22.

140 *Id.* at 737.

141 *Id.* at 741.

142 *See* discussion of this case at *supra* notes 90-94.

Lipscomb was contacted several times by the reporter but refused to comment.[143]

The state supreme court, however, found the newspaper negligent primarily because Cox did not interview students friendly to Lipscomb. Though recognizing that the story contained information favorable to the teacher,[144] and that Cox repeatedly attempted to interview Lipscomb and her superiors to learn their side of the controversy,[145] the court found ample evidence of negligence.[146]

There was insufficient evidence of actual malice, however. Lipscomb made six claims to support her charge that the newspaper published the story with actual malice, but the court rejected all six:[147]

(1) Lipscomb claimed that the ill will of the reporter's sources raised obvious doubts as to their veracity, but the court found the only bias was due to their dissatisfaction with Lipscomb as a teacher, and there was nothing to impeach their credibility.

(2) Lipscomb claimed Cox was predisposed against her, but evidence to support the charge was insufficient.

(3) Lipscomb claimed that Cox resolved ambiguities against her and omitted favorable information, but the court held that, while some favorable information may have been omitted, the

---

143 362 S.E.2d 32, 34-35 (Va. 1987).

144 *Id.* at 40.

145 *Id.* at 41.

146 *Id.* at 38.

147 *Id.* at 38-42.

story contained positive, as well as negative, information.

(4) Lipscomb claimed that the newspaper should have been held to a high degree of accountability because of the absence of deadline pressure. The court noted that in each case she cited to support her argument, however, there was evidence of other reckless conduct absent from the *Richmond Newspapers* case.

(5) The court rejected Lipscomb's claim that the newspaper's decision to wait and publish the story when Cox returned to the office from a vacation was evidence of serious doubts as to the truth of the story. The fact that the newspaper wanted to double check some of the information was hardly evidence of serious doubts, the court held.

(6) There was no evidence to support Lipscomb's claim that Cox threatened her or her principal. "On the contrary," the court held, "the evidence shows that Cox was trying to persuade them to give Lipscomb's side of the controversy."[148]

What is remarkable about the *Richmond Newspapers* case is that, based on these findings, the court was able to find evidence of even negligence. The court recognized that Cox's witnesses were unimpeachable, that he had repeatedly attempted to interview Lipscomb and her superiors, and that he included favorable information about her in the story. Yet, because the court decided Cox did not interview enough sources from a specific category, the court found the newspaper negligent. The Virginia Supreme Court was taking on a role that the U.S. Supreme Court

---

[148] *Id.* at 41.

has specifically eschewed – the role of editor. The First Amendment, the Court has held, stands as a barrier against "intrusion into the function of editors."[149]

And, in *Fleming v. Moore* – the last of the cases settled in *Gazette* – the court held
that a real estate developer "abandoned all judgment and reason" in making comments about a university professor during a controversy over a housing development.[150] The developer placed an advertisement in the student newspaper at the University of Virginia, in which he called the professor a racist, said he was being supported on the public dole at the expense of the "working people," and said the professor's stated grounds for opposing the development were a sham to conceal his effort to oppress blacks. The court held that the developer placed the ad, with insufficient evidence, to intimidate the professor in order to eliminate him as a voice of opposition.[151] This, the court held, was evidence of actual malice.

Similarly, when Humberto Pujals Jr. of Government Micro Resources, after firing Alan W. Jackson, reported that Jackson had lost the company $3 million, Pujals, the court held, knew his statement

---

[149] *See, e.g.,* Miami Herald v. Tornillo, 418 U.S. 241, 258 (1974). *See also id.* at 261 (White, J., concurring); Nebraska Press Ass'n v. Stuart, 427 U.S. 539, 613 (Brennan, J., concurring).

[150] Gazette v. Harris, 325 S.E.2d 713, 746 (Va. 1985).

[151] *Id.* at 725.

was false. The company had lost $3 million, but it wasn't all because of Jackson.[152]

Two other cases demonstrate the state supreme court's low threshold for fault in libel cases. In *Newspaper Publishing Corp. v. Burke* the court held that a newspaper article may have been published with actual malice when a journalist attributed controversial statements to a source who denied making the statements.[153] An aggravating circumstance was the fact that the journalist promised the source an opportunity to check the story before publication, but failed to keep the promise, even in light of a second source doubting the accuracy of the information.[154]

The state supreme court also found the possibility of knowledge of falsity in a case involving WJLA-TV, a Washington, D.C., station that broadcasts into Virginia. The court held that a trial court did not err when it presented the question of actual malice to a jury in a defamation case against the station brought by Dr. Stephen M. Levin, an orthopedist. The station broadcast what it advertised as an investigative piece based on complaints that Levin exercised what was tantamount to sexual assault in his treatment of a number of women.[155] The station broadcast remarks by another physician, Dr. Loren Fishman, who had called Levin's treatment improper, but who had

---

[152] Gov't Micro Resources, Inc. v. Jackson, 624 S.E.2d 63, 68, 70 (Va. 2006).

[153] 224 S.E.2d 132, 137 (1976). *See also* Fitzgerald v. Penthouse, Inc., 691 F.2d 666 (4th Cir. 1982).

[154] *Id.*

[155] WJLA-TV v. Levin, 564 S.E.2d 383, 386-87 (Va. 2002). *See discussion* accompanying *supra* notes 31-32.

retracted those statements after receiving additional information. In addition, WJLA accused Levin of committing criminal sexual assault knowing that he had not been charged and that, based upon the results of an investigation by the board of medicine, they probably could not be sustained. These failings were evidence of actual malice, the court held.[156]

Finally, following the lead of the U.S. Supreme Court, the state high court has held that the simple failure to investigate is not sufficient evidence of actual malice.

Tommy Jackson, a candidate for house of delegates, sued editorial writer Dennis A. Hartig and Landmark Communications Inc., owners of the *Virginian-Pilot,* for an editorial endorsing Jackson's opponent, based in part on Jackson's term on the Virginia Beach School Board. Jackson was indicted when the board went over budget, but was acquitted. During his unsuccessful bid for city council, the *Virginian-Pilot* endorsed him.[157] The later editorial misstated some of the facts related to the school board budget issue, which had been correctly reported in the earlier editorial. The court found that there was no actual malice simply because correct information existed in the newspapers files and Hartig failed to look at those files.[158]

---

[156] *Id.* at 392.

[157] Jackson v. Hartig, 645 S.E.2d 303, 305-06 (Va. 2007).

[158] *Id.* at 308-09 (citing St. Amant v. Thompson, 390 U.S. 727, 731 (1968). *See also* Jordan v. Kollman, 612 S.E.2d 203, 210 (Va. 2005) (holding that a citizen's reliance on a newspaper article in preparing an advertisement that contained

Virginia courts, it seems, are taking a dim view of inaccuracies published about persons who assume roles of innocent victims. The *Richmond Newspapers* case and the three negligence cases in the *Gazette* opinion demonstrate that the Virginia Supreme Court has a low threshold when determining the existence of fault. While appearing to rely on the "reasonable journalist" definition of negligence, the court seems to be applying a much stricter test. The action by the reporter in *Richmond Newspapers,* in particular, was reasonable.

On the other hand, the court seems to be applying the actual malice standard with the rigor that the U.S. Supreme Court requires. Evidence of thorough research before publishing is insulating the media from liability.

THE LIBEL DEFENDANT

A defendant can win a libel action in a number of ways. The defendant, by making a variety of arguments, can attempt to have a case dismissed by the judge before the trial begins. This is called seeking a summary judgment. Arguments for summary judgment can also be made at the completion of the plaintiff's case. At that point, the defendant can argue that the plaintiff has not satisfied all elements of the burden of proof and, therefore, the case should be dismissed. This argument would come after the defendant's attorney has cross-examined the plaintiff's

---

falsehoods about a candidate for public office precludes a finding of actual malice).

witnesses in an attempt to demonstrate weaknesses in the evidence presented by the plaintiff.

A defendant is not required to produce evidence, but if efforts to dismiss a case are unsuccessful, the defendant will almost always do so. That evidence can either attack elements in the plaintiff's case or can advance a defense for the publication. Virginia law provides for three complete defenses for libel: expiration of the statute of limitations, qualified privilege and opinion. The opinion defense can be sub-divided into the publication of pure opinion and the privilege of fair comment and criticism.

Truth is probably a complete defense as well. Since a libel plaintiff must prove the defamatory material is false, if a defendant can introduce evidence that the published material is true, the defendant will win. The Virginia Supreme Court, however, has said that, since the plaintiff must prove falsity, "[T]ruth no longer is an affirmative defense to be established by the defendant."[159] But a defendant who wants to advance a defense of truth would almost surely be allowed to do so, particularly since federal courts in Virginia have continued to hold that truth is a complete defense within the commonwealth.[160]

In addition, the developing defenses of good reporting and neutral reporting may protect journalists from some libel verdicts.

---

[159] Gazette v. Harris, 325 S.E.2d 713, 725 (Va. 1985).

[160] *See* cases cited at *infra* note 216.

Statute of Limitations

When it applies, the statute of limitations defense stops a libel action before the trial begins. Virginia, like most states, only allows recent disputes to be adjudicated. Statutes of limitations provide specific deadlines in which legal actions can be filed.

The statute of limitations for libel in Virginia is one year, so no libel action can be brought based on a publication that is more than a year old.[161] The clock begins running on a libel action when the publication is generally available to the public, rather than from the copyright date or the date that may appear on the publication.[162]

In addition, the Fourth U.S. Circuit Court of Appeals has held that the single-publication rule applies in Virginia.[163] In essence, the rule prohibits a libel plaintiff from maintaining more than one libel action against the same defendant based on one publication. In the absence of such a rule, a plaintiff could sue the defendant for libel in every circuit in Virginia where the defamatory material was circulated.

Qualified Privilege

The privilege to make certain communications has a long and honorable history in the commonwealth. Early in the twentieth century, the Virginia Supreme Court recognized that citizens have

---

161 VA. CODE ANN. § 8.01-247.1 (1950).

162 *See* Morrisey v. William Morrow & Co., Inc., 739 F.2d 962, 967-68 (4th Cir. 1984).

163 *Id.*

a privilege – or right – to comment on matters of public concern, that these commentators should be informed about such matters, and that the conduct of public officers or candidates for public office is a matter of public concern.[164]

Through the years, then, there developed two type of privilege: absolute and qualified.

Absolutely privileged communications are those made in the course of conducting government business. The Virginia Supreme Court has held that it attaches to three classes of communication: (1) proceedings of legislative bodies, (2) judicial proceedings, and (3) communications by military and naval officers.[165] As will be demonstrated, it's clear that other types of public proceedings are also privileged. An absolute privilege means that no lawsuits can arise from statements made as part of the official proceedings. A member of the Virginia General Assembly, for example, can say anything from the chamber floor without fear of a defamation action. And a member of a city council or board of supervisors cannot be sued for libel based on comments made during an official meeting. In addition, documents that arise from these official settings are privileged.

Qualified privilege grew out of a recognition that speech on certain matters needed to be protected. Originally, in addition to protection for governmental proceedings, the law also protected "anything said or written by a master in giving the character of a servant

---

[164] James v. Haymes, 178 S.E. 18, 19-20 (Va. 1935).

[165] Storey v. Norfolk-Portsmouth Newspapers, Inc., 118 S.E.2d 668, 669 (Va. 1961).

who has been in employment."[166] Privilege, then, was specifically designed to attach to communications between persons who owed some duty to each other.

Early in the twentieth century, however, the commonwealth recognized that the discussion of public events is important to society. Indeed, there was a duty of sorts between public officials and citizens and between citizens and other citizens related to the conduct of the public's business, justifying the extension of the qualified privilege to reports and discussion of public events. A qualified privilege means that persons reporting on or discussing the events that occur in absolutely privileged forums are protected from libel suits if certain qualifications are met. Those qualifications are that the report must be accurate, it must be fair, and it must be made without ill will or spite, that is, without common law malice.

An important corollary to the qualified privilege rule is that, in addition to official proceedings, it attaches to reports taken from public records. The privilege attaches even if the record is in error and, therefore, a report based on the record is in error. Truth or falsity, therefore, is not at issue in such cases. The question is whether "the news article was published in good faith and was a substantially correct report of the record. . . ."[167] If the news account is not an accurate representation of what is in the official

---

[166] Penick v. Ratcliffe, 140 S.E. 664, 669 (Va. 1927) (quoting Williams Printing Co. v. Saunders, 73 S.E. 472 (Va. 1912)).

[167] *Id.*

record, however, the journalist may be held accountable.[168]

Qualified privilege has been held to attach to various reports from sources that were not governmental. For example:

- Statements by a college public information officer to a newspaper reporter about a controversy on campus were conceded by attorneys in the case to be privileged.[169]
- A press release by a plaintiff in a lawsuit stating that the suit had been filed and accurately summarizing the allegations in the suit was held to be privileged.[170]
- A motorist's complaint to a police chief about the conduct of a police officer was held to be privileged.[171]
- Because the law recognizes that privilege attaches to communications between parties who have common interests, communications between employers and employees and among employees in the same company have been held to be privileged.[172]

---

[168] *See* Times-Dispatch Publ'g Co., Inc. v. Zoll, 139 S.E. 505, 507 (Va. 1927).

[169] Sanders v. Harris (Times-World Corp.), 192 S.E.2d 754, 757 (Va. 1972).

[170] Bull v. Logetronics, Inc., 323 F. Supp. 115, 135 (E.D. Va. 1971).

[171] Smalls v. Wright, 399 S.E.2d 805 (Va. 1991).

[172] Kroger Co. v. Young, 172 S.E.2d 720, 722-23 (Va. 1970); Montgomery Ward v. Nance, 182 S.E. 264, 269-70 (Va. 1935).

- Communications among faculty and administrators at Radford University about a tenure case were held to be qualifiedly privileged.[173]

The qualified privilege defense can be defeated on a showing that the published report was inaccurate, unfair, or was made with ill will or spite. Specifically, it may be defeated upon a showing of actual malice, use of intemperate or disproportionate language, deliberate over-exposure of the charges or over-publicity, or gross indifference.[174] It may not be defeated upon a showing of negligence.[175] The official record need not be quoted verbatim, and some minor errors will not defeat the privilege, but the report must be substantially correct.[176] In addition, if a journalist draws inferences from the report and those inferences are incorrect, the privilege will not stand.[177] Finally, privilege does not extend to official reports of acts by foreign governments.[178]

---

[173] Lideman v. Lesnick, 604 S.E.2d 55 (Va. 2004).

[174] *See* Great Coastal Express, Inc. v. Ellington, 334 S.E.2d 846, 853 (Va. 1985); Southwestern Tidewater Opportunity Project, Inc. v. Bade, 435 S.E.2d 131 (Va. 1993).

[175] *See* Gazette v. Harris, 325 S.E.2d 713, 727 (Va. 1985). *See also* Rushford v. New Yorker Magazine, 846 F.2d 249, 254-55 (4th Cir. 1988).

[176] *See* Alexandria Gazette Corp. v. West, 93 S.E.2d 274, 279 (Va. 1956). *See also Rushford,* 846 F.2d at 254-55.

[177] *See* Times-Dispatch Publ'g, Inc. v. Zoll, 139 S.E. 505, 507-08 (Va. 1927).

[178] *See* Lee v. The Dong-A-Ilbo, 849 F.2d 876, 877-80 (4th Cir. 1988).

One additional privilege exists for broadcasters in Virginia. A state law provides that a broadcaster cannot be held responsible for defamatory statements made over the air by someone who does not work for the station. The privilege can be defeated if a plaintiff can show that the broadcaster failed to exercise due care to prevent the broadcast of the defamation. The same statute provides that a broadcaster cannot be held liable for defamatory statements made by or on behalf of any candidate for public office under any circumstances.[179]

Opinion

Statements of opinion are protected in one of two ways in Virginia. First, if a statement is considered pure opinion – that is, it cannot be proved to be true or false – it is not considered defamatory and, therefore, is not actionable. Second, if reasonable people can disagree on the truth or falsity of a statement, and if the statement is based on facts that are provably true or false, the statement is considered fair comment or criticism and is protected when certain qualifications are met.

Pure Opinion. Virginia protects pure opinion as a category of speech even though the U.S. Supreme Court has ruled that such protection is not necessary under the First Amendment. In *Milkovich v. Lorain Journal,*[180] the Court held that statements of opinion are not part of a special category of speech that is automatically protected. However, the Court also

---

[179] VA. CODE ANN. §8.01-49 (1950).

[180] 497 U.S. 1 (1990).

noted that a statement cannot be defamatory unless it can be proved to be false.[181] Under *Milkovich,* therefore, statements of opinion are implicitly protected, since they cannot be proved to be false.

The *Milkovich* ruling requires an additional step in libel actions involving opinion. Virginia has circumvented that extra step. In 1985, the Virginia Supreme Court ruled that "pure expressions of opinion, not amounting to 'fighting words' cannot form the basis of an action for defamation."[182] The ruling was based on the First Amendment to the U.S. Constitution and on Article 1, section 12, of Virginia's constitution.[183] These two provisions, the court held, "[P]rotect the right of the people to teach, preach, write, or speak any such opinion, however ill-founded, without inhibition by actions for libel and slander." Then, quoting from Thomas Jefferson's first inaugural address in 1801, the Virginia court noted that "'error of

---

[181] *Id.* at 19-20.

[182] Chaves v. Johnson, 335 S.E.2d 97, 101-02 (Va. 1985).

[183] Article 1, § 12 of the Virginia Constitution reads:

> That the freedom of speech and of the press are among the great bulwarks of liberty, and can never be restrained except by despotic governments; that any citizen may freely speak, write, and publish his sentiments on all subjects, being responsible for the abuse of that right; that the General Assembly shall not pass any law abridging the freedom of speech or of the press, nor the right of the people peaceably to assemble, and to petition the government for a redress of grievances.

opinion may be tolerated where reason is left free to combat it.'"[184]

Courts have generally provided protection for opinion on the basis of three distinct rationales: (1) an idea that cannot be false cannot be true and, in a libel action, the constitutional defense of truth would be lost; (2) an opinion carries less authority than a fact and is less likely to threaten the interests and values safeguarded by libel law; and (3) most forms of speech have an affirmative constitutional value, and a rule that chills the expression of opinion is unacceptable.[185] The point is, only statements of fact are defamatory – what one believes is not.

The Virginia Supreme Court, for example, has held that to call someone inexperienced is a statement of opinion and, therefore, does not impute unfitness. Noted the court: "Many physicians, it is to be hoped, cure their first patients." The court also noted that the characterization, like all statements of opinion, is relative: "A corporal might seem inexperienced to a sergeant, but not to a private. The relative nature of such opinions is obvious to anyone who hears them."[186]

Other statements of opinion, Virginia courts have held, are:

- that a person or agency charges excessive fees for its services.[187]

---

[184] *Chaves,* 335 S.E.2d at 102.

[185] Potomac Valve & Fitting, Inc. v. Crawford Fitting Co., 829 F.2d 1280, 1285-86 (4th Cir. 1988).

[186] *Chaves,* 335 S.E.2d at 101.

[187] *Id.*

- that a person is discourteous;[188]
- that a charitable organization does not spend a reasonable percent of its total income on program services;[189]
- the statement, "[P]ersonally I wouldn't trust him as far as I can throw him;"[190]
- a statement that physicians were unprofessional or unethical.[191]
- the characterization on a radio program that a named person was "the ugliest man in Danville;"[192]
- characterizing the operator of a program to distribute gift packs to service personnel as a "veteran charity entrepreneur" who charged "hefty" markups for the gift packs;[193]
- a criticism that a contractor would not finish a road on time because of the contractor's past performance;[194]

---

188 Auvil v. Times-Journal Co., 10 Media L. Rep. (BNA) 2302, 2303 (E.D. Va. 1984).

189 Nat'l Found. for Cancer Research v. Council for Better Business Bureaus, Inc., 705 F.2d 98, 100-01 (4th Cir. 1983).

190 Lapkoff v. Wilks, 969 F.2d 78, 82 (4th Cir. 1992).

191 Fuste v. Riverside Healthcare Ass'n, Inc., 575 S.E.2d 858, 860 (Va. 2003).

192 Motsinger v. Kelly, 11 Media L. Rep. (BNA) 2459, 2460 (Danville Cir. Ct., Aug. 12, 1985).

193 Chapin v. Knight-Ridder, Inc., 993 F.2d 1087, 1093-94 (4th Cir. 1993).

194 James v. Haymes, 178 S.E. 18, 22 (Va. 1935).

- a statement that there was a problem with an auto dealership's sales manager who either did not know about a credit fraud problem or did nothing about the problem;[195]
- a statement that a person was unfit to be a Scoutmaster.[196]

On the other hand, the Virginia Supreme Court determined that, while statements about sexual harassment might be statements of opinion, a statement that a person received negative performance evaluations because of the person's responses to so-called sexual harassment was a statement of fact,[197] as was calling a person who crossed a picket line a traitor.[198] Other statements that were held to be statements of fact are:

- that physicians had abandoned their patients and might also be incompetent;[199]
- that the owner of a construction company was going to "screw" a client;[200]
- that an attorney "just takes peoples' money" and clients would receive more money in disputes with

---

195 *Lapkoff,* 969 F.2d at 82-83.

196 Gibson v. Boy Scouts of America, 163 Fed. Appx. 206, 213 (4th Cir. 2006).

197 Williams v. Garraghty, 455 S.E.2d 209, 215 (Va. 1995).

198 Old Dominion Branch 496 v. Austin, 192 S.E.2d 737, 742 (Va. 1972), *rev'd* 418 U.S. 264 (1974). *See* discussion accompanying *infra* notes 189-93.

199 Fueste v. Riverside Healthcare Ass'n, Inc., 575 S.E.2d 858, 858 (Va. 2003).

200 Tharpe v. Saunders, 737 S.E.2d 890, 891-92 (Va. 2013).

insurance companies than if the attorney represented them;[201]

Often, particularly when professional disputes are involved, libel cases contain both statements of fact and statements of opinion. For example, when Cynthia Hyland was terminated from her position with Raytheon Technical Services, she sued on a number of grounds, including defamation based on five statements made in a performance evaluation. The points made in the evaluation and the rulings of the Virginia Supreme Court were:[202]

- that Hyghland and her team were off plan on a number of financial targets by specific percentages was a statement of fact; an earlier statement that the team was "significantly" off plan would have been a statement of opinion;
- that Hyghland was responsible for certain losses that adversely affected the company was a statement of fact;
- that Hyghland was "frequently verbose and vocal in her opinions" to the point of inhibiting discussion by others was a statement of opinion;
- that Hyghland appeared to be unwilling to accept and work with feedback was a statement of opinion;

---

[201] Tronfeld v. Nationwide Mutual Ins. Co., 636 S.E.2d 447 (Va. 2006).

[202] Raytheon Technical Services Co. v. Hyland, 641 S.E.2d 84, 90-92 (Va. 2007).

- a statement that Hyland was inappropriately and openly critical of supervisors and peers in the company and that such behavior was destructive was a statement of both fact and opinion – that she was openly critical of others was a statement of fact, but that the statements were inappropriate was a statement of opinion.

Similarly, when anesthesiologist Bradley Cashion sued surgeon Robert Smith for a critical assessment of how Cashion handled a patient who died, the court found some of Smith's statements to be factual and others to be opinion. Smith's statements that Cashion made "a very poor effort," "didn't really try" and gave up on the patient were held to be statements of opinion; the statmemtnts that the patient could have survived with better resuscitation, that Cashion "determined from the beginning that [the patient] wasn't going to make it," and that Cashion euthanized the patient were statements of fact.[203]

In libel actions, the responsibility is upon the court, rather than a jury, to determine whether a statement is one of fact or opinion.[204]

Fair Comment & Criticism. Fair comment and criticism is a qualified privilege that protects commentary based on statements of fact. In 1935, the Virginia Supreme Court explained the rationale behind the privilege:

> The privilege or right of a citizen to comment on matters of public concern is based upon a

---

[203] Cashion v. Smith, 749 S.E.2d 526, 531 (Va. 2013).

[204] Chaves v. Johnson, 335 S.E.2d 97, 102 (Va. 1985).

> sound public policy, i.e., the public should be informed of the character, qualifications, actions, and conduct of public officers and candidates for public offices, and other matters of public nature. . . . The comment or criticism in such cases may reflect upon the plaintiff in his public actions or conduct; indeed, he would not complain unless they tended in some degree to defame or ridicule him. Sound public policy requires that immunity should be granted to newspapers and other citizens in the discussion of public affairs and where the comment or stricture is based upon established facts, an action does not lie unless there is proof of. . . malice, or the language used so exceeds reasonable limits that malice may be inferred therefrom.[205]

For the defense to succeed in Virginia, therefore, the comment (1) must be on matters of public concern, (2) must be based upon statements of fact that are accurately stated, and (3) must be made without common law malice, that is, without ill will, hatred or spite. Courts in many jurisdictions also require that a comment be the genuine opinion of the publisher of the comment. That is, the comment or criticism must be the expression of the publisher's opinion, it cannot be a news account relating the opinion of another. While this element has not been explicitly adopted in Virginia, it appears to be implicit the court's rulings.

---

[205] James v. Hayes, 178 S.E. 18, 20 (Va. 1935).

Fair comment and criticism is often easier to define than to apply. In one Virginia case, for example, a court held that criticism of a fund-raising agency for not spending enough of its income on program services was a statement of opinion and protected.[206] To report that a bank was near insolvency, however, was a statement of fact rather than opinion, even though the statement was an interpretation based upon an analysis of the bank's holdings.[207]

One of the most famous disagreements over whether a statement was opinion or fact grew out of a Virginia case that was ultimately settled by the U.S. Supreme Court. The case began during a labor dispute. A non-union post office employee complained about being identified in a union newsletter as a "scab."[208] When he asked for a definition of the word "scab," the newsletter published the following, which is often attributed to Jack London:

> After God had finished the rattlesnake, the toad, and the vampire, He had some awful substance left with which he made a scab.
>
> A scab is a two-legged animal with a corkscrew soul, a water brain, a combination

---

[206] Nat'l Foundation for Cancer Research v. Council for Better Business Bureaus, Inc., 705 F.2d 98, 100 (4th Cir. 1983).

[207] Blue Ridge Bank v. Veribanc, 866 F.2d 681, 865 (4th Cir. 1989).

[208] Old Dominion Branch 496 v. Austin, 192 S.E.2d 737, 738-39 (Va. 1972), *rev'd* 418 U.S. 264 (1974).

> backbone of jelly and glue. Where others have hearts, he carries a tumor of rotten principles.
>
> When a scab comes down the street, men turn their backs and Angels weep in Heaven, and the Devil shuts the gates of hell to keep him out.
>
> No man (or woman) has a right to scab so long as there is a pool of water to drown his carcass in, or a rope long enough to hang his body with. Judas was a gentleman compared with a scab. For betraying his Master, he had character enough to hang himself. A scab has not.
>
> Essau sold his birthright for a mess of pottage. Judas sold his Savior for thirty pieces of silver. Benedict Arnold sold his country for a promise of a commission in the British Army. The scab sells his birthright, country, his wife, his children and his fellowmen for an unfulfilled promise from his employer.
>
> Essau was a traitor to himself; judas was a traitor to God; Benedict Arnold was a traitor to his country, a SCAB is a traitor to his god, his country, his family and his class.[209]

The Virginia Supreme Court ruled that identifying persons who crossed picket lines as traitors of such low character and rotten principles that they should be despised by their fellow workers was not a statement of opinion and, therefore, was not protected by the First Amendment.[210]

---

[209] *Id.* at 739.

[210] *Id.* at 742.

The U.S. Supreme Court, however, reversed the ruling, holding that the piece consisted of "rhetorical hyperbole" and was "a lusty and imaginative expression of contempt felt by union members towards those who refuse to join."[211] No one, the Court noted, would reasonably believe that there was a charge of the criminal offense of treason.[212]

Truth

Truth has long been recognized as a complete defense for defamation.[213]

In 1986, however, the U.S. Supreme Court made explicit what had been implicit in libel law since its landmark ruling in *New York Times Co. v. Sullivan.* In *New York Times,* of course, the Court ruled that actual malice was defined as "knowledge of falsity," the implication being that there must be falsity before there can be "knowledge" of the falsity. In *Philadelphia Newspapers v. Hepps,* the Court stated explicitly that falsity must be proved by the plaintiff in libel actions when the subject of the allegedly defamatory material relates to matters of public concern.[214]

The ruling, and the implicit collateral holding that the knowledge of false statements must also be

---

[211] Letter Carriers v. Austin, 418 U.S. 264, 286 (1974). The name of the case changed when it was decided by the U.S. Supreme Court.

[212] *Id.* at 285.

[213] *See, e.g.,* Chaffin v. Lynch, 1 S.E. 803, 807 (Va. 1887).

[214] 475 U.S. 767 (1986).

proved, prompted the Virginia Supreme Court, as indicated previously, to hold that truth is no longer a defense. Since the plaintiff is required to prove falsity in order to establish the negligence of such falsity, the state supreme court reasoned, "[T]ruth is no longer an affirmative defense to be established by the defendant."[215]

The ruling is probably more semantic than precedential, however. It is inconceivable that a defendant in a libel action would not be allowed to defend on the ground that the defamatory statement is true. In addition, even in the face of the state supreme court's ruling, the federal appellate courts in Virginia have continued to hold to the tenet that truth is a complete defense in libel actions.[216]

When truth has been pleaded in libel actions, the court has held that slight inaccuracies will not cause the defense to fail. So long as the defamatory charge is true in substance, the defense will stand.[217]

Good Reporting, Neutral Reporting

A couple of developing defenses should be mentioned before discussion of the defendant's case is closed. The defenses of good reporting and neutral

---

[215] Gazette v. Harris, 325 S.E.2d 713, 725 (Va. 1985).

[216] *See, e.g.,* McBride v. City of Roanoke Redevelopment and Housing Auth., 871 F. Supp. 885, 891-92 (W.D. Va. 1994); Bills v. Sunshine Wireless Co., 824 F. Supp. 60, 64 (E.D. Va. 1993); Chapin v. Greve, 787 F. Supp. 557, 563 (E.D. Va. 1992); Seabolt v. Westmoreland Coal Co., 703 F. Supp. 1235, 1242 (W.D. Va. 1989), *aff'd* 898 F.2d 144 (4th Cir. 1990).=

[217] Saleeby v. Free Press, Inc., 91 S.E.2d 405, 407 (Va. 1956).

reporting have not been explicitly applied in Virginia, but have been implied in a number of court cases.

Good Reporting. The defense grows out of the Supreme Court's pronouncement that no libel plaintiff may prevail without showing some degree of fault[218] and a Virginia statute providing that a showing of proper investigation, reliability of sources, and absence of negligence would mitigate damages.[219] The defense is based on the presumption that if there is no showing of negligence, there can be no showing of fault of any kind, and the defendant will prevail. Since negligence is the minimum degree of fault, no greater degree of fault can exist if the minimum degree does not exist.[220]

To demonstrate an absence of negligence, a news organization must demonstrate that it properly investigated the defamatory allegations before publishing. This means contacting all relevant persons involved in the controversy, particularly the subject of the defamation, using documents when possible, quoting accurately and clearly following the guidelines of responsible reporting.[221] Basically it means providing a good faith effort to be accurate and fair.

Neutral Reporting. Neutral reporting is an extension of qualified privilege – it provides protection for journalists who report newsworthy comments even

---

[218] Gertz v. Welch, 418 U.S. 323, 347-48 (1974).

[219] VA. CODE ANN. § 8-01-48 (1950).

[220] *See supra* note 132.

[221] *See, e.g.*, HOPKINS, *supra* note 122, at 18-20.

though they may doubt the truth of those comments. The privilege attaches when:[222]

- newsworthy comments
- are made by a responsible and prominent individual or organization
- about a public figure
- and are reported accurately.

The defense has not been recognized in either Virginia or the Fourth Circuit, but it has come close. A federal court in South Carolina has recognized the privilege, and the Fourth Circuit gave a nod to that ruling in a case out of Virginia.

In *Sunshine Sportswear & Electronics, Inc. v. WSOC Television, Inc.,*[223] the federal court for the District of South Carolina dismissed a libel action brought against a television station that broadcast a story focusing on consumer complaints against the camera retailer. The station presented an accurate representation of the complaints, the court held, along with the response to the allegations and was, therefore, protected by the privilege of neutral reporting.[224]

Four years later, the Fourth Circuit noted the decision by the district court, but declined an opportunity to recognize the privilege in the circuit. The case began when Roger Chapin, the president of a company that raised money in order to send gift packages to American soldiers in Saudi Arbia, sued the Knight-Ridder corporation for a story published in the

---

[222] *See* Edwards v. National Audubon Soc'y, Inc., 556 F.2d 113, 120 (2d Cir. 1977).

[223] 738 F. Supp. 1499 (D.S.C. 1989).

[224] *Id.* at 1511.

Philadelphia Inquirer and other papers owned by the company critical of the operations of Chapin's company.[225]

The court ruled in favor of Knight-Ridder, but not because of the neutral reporting privilege. "[W]e need not cast our lot one way or another," on neutral reporting, the court held, because the case "fits within the 'fair report' privilege.'"[226]

Mitigating Damages

Virginia law provides that a defendant may mitigate damages by offering an apology to the plaintiff[227] or by producing evidence showing that the news story was responsibly investigated, written and published.[228] The viability of this last statute under modern libel law is in question, however. Since the U.S. Supreme Court has required all libel plaintiffs to prove some degree of fault in order to win their cases, a showing that there is no negligence will usually be sufficient for a libel defendant to win. Negligence is based directly on how a story was investigated, written and published, and since a showing that there is no negligence is sufficient for a defendant to win, the statute may have little meaning today.

---

[225] Chapin v. Knight-Ridder, Inc., 993 F.2d 1087, 1091 (4th Cir. 1087).

[226] *Id.* at 1097. The court had recognized the fair report privilege, also called "qualified privilege" in *Reuber v. Food Chemical News, Inc.,* 925 F.2d 703 (4th Cir. 1991), a Maryland case.

[227] VA. CODE ANN. § 8.01-46 (1950).

[228] VA. CODE ANN. § 8.01-48 (1950).

6. PRIVATE PEOPLE, PRIVATE PLACES AND PEACE OF MIND

Invasion of privacy is a relatively recent but an emotion-charged area of the law. The publication of some secret tidbit or a camera probing into private places can bring the most vociferous denunciations of the media. Few publications raise the ire of the public more than a photograph of a grieving mother or a story about events from a person's private life.

Partly because of the high emotions associated with the conflict between a person's private life and newsgathering, a body of law has developed in the United States to protect the privacy rights of individuals. That body of law was first explored in detail by William Prosser in 1965 as part of the American Law Institute's *Restatement of the Law* series.[1] In the *Restatement (Second) of Torts,* Prosser identified four types of invasion of privacy:

---

[1] Invasion of privacy traces its heritage to 1890 when Samuel Warren and Louis Brandeis published "The Right of Privacy" in the *Harvard Law Review.* Prosser, however, was first to systematically examine the law of invasion of privacy and delineate the four separate invasion of privacy torts. *See* RESTATEMENT (SECOND) OF TORTS § 652A, comment a (1977); William L. Prosser, *Privacy*, 48 CAL. L. REV. 343 (1960); Samuel Warren & Louis Brandeis, *The Right to Privacy*, 4 HARVARD L. REV. 193 (1890). Some portions of The RESTATEMENT OF TORTS are now in its third edition.

appropriation, intrusion, publication of private information and false light invasion of privacy.[2]

Since then, a number of states have sifted out some of these torts. Several states do not allow lawsuits to be brought under the tort of false light invasion of privacy, for example.[3] Virginia has gone even further: The commonwealth recognizes only appropriation, and only twice have appellate courts in Virginia resolved appropriation cases.[4]

This does not mean that Virginia lawmakers have no regard for the privacy and peace of mind of individuals, however. Indeed, vestiges of intrusion, false light and publication of private information appear in a variety of forms in Virginia law. The commonwealth has also made ample effort to protect the privacy or peace of mind of its citizens through statutes prohibiting insulting words, the intentional infliction of emotional distress, trespassing and the like. In addition, in 1976, the Virginia General Assembly passed the Privacy Protection Act, which

---

[2] RESTATEMENT (SECOND) OF TORTS § 652A (1977) (hereinafter RESTATEMENT).

[3] Some of those states are Florida, Massachusetts, New York, North Carolina and Texas. *See* Jews for Jesus, Inc. v. Rapp, 997 So.2d 1098 (Fla. 2008); Elm Medical Laboratory v. RKO General, Inc., 532 N.E. 2d 675 (Mass. 1989); Costanza v. Seinfeld, 693 N.Y.S.2d 897 (N.Y. Sup. Ct. 1999); Renwick v. News and Observer Publishing Co., 312 S.E.2d 405 (N.C. 1984); Cain v. Hearst Corp., 878 S.W.2d 577 (Tex. 1994).

[4] *See* Falwell v. Penthouse Int'l, Ltd., 521 F. Supp. 1204 (W.D. Va. 1981); Town & Country Properties, Inc. v. Riggins, 457 S.E.2d 356 (Va. 1995). The two appropriation cases are discussed at *infra* notes 13-14 and 17-19.

doesn't protect privacy, but regulates the way information about individuals is collected, manipulated and disseminated. The act focuses on data collection agencies rather than the dissemination of information by the individuals or the media. It gives individuals the right of access to information collected about them.[5]

Many of these statutes are not typically regarded as "invasion of privacy" statutes, but because their design is to protect the privacy, dignity or peace of mind of individuals, they will be addressed in this chapter, along with a passel of related issues. Since the mid-2000s, Virginia statutes have been more specific in protecting Internet privacy. Virginia's privacy statutes recognize the role of computers in maintaining and disseminating private information. Because of that, government entities must meet certain statutory requirements to properly maintain and protect sensitive private information regarding commonwealth citizens. These regulations even include mandatory disclosures to commonwealth citizens regarding how their information will be maintained, protected, and used by state agencies.[6]

APPROPRIATION

Appropriation is the use of a person's name, image or likeness for commercial gain without

---

[5] *See* VA. CODE ANN. §§ 2.2-3800-2.2-3809 (1950).

[6] *See* VA. CODE ANN. §§ 2.2-3800; 2.2-3803; 2.2-3806 (1950).

permission.[7] In Virginia an appropriation suit may be brought by:

> [A]ny person whose name, portrait, or picture is used without having first obtained the written consent of such person, or if dead, of the surviving consort and if none, of the next of kin, or if a minor, the written consent of his or her parent or guardian, for advertising purposes or for the purposes of trade.[8]

The statute allows a suit to be brought up until twenty years after the death of the person whose name or image is used.

The Virginia Supreme Court has construed the state's appropriation statute as granting a property right to individuals.[9] That is, according to the court, a person's name, likeness or image is tantamount to a piece of property, and only the individual can benefit from the use of that property. Therefore, an action for appropriation "is an action for invasion of. . . 'property' rights and not one for 'injury to the person.'"[10]

Appropriation most often applies to advertising, where images of the beautiful or well-

---

[7] RESTATEMENT, *supra* note 2, at § 652C.

[8] VA. CODE ANN. §8.01-40 (1950).

[9] *See* Lavery v. Automation Mgmt. Consultants, Inc., 360 S.E.2d 336 (Va. 1987).

[10] *Id.* at 341-42.

known are used to sell products. One had best have the permission of Michael Jordan before putting his photograph on a box of Wheaties or in an advertisement for Nike basketball shoes, for example.

Appropriation can also apply to free-lance photographers and writers, however, who make their livings selling information or images. Virtually any time a free-lance photographer sells a photo to a newspaper or magazine, for example, the photographer has used the likeness of a person for commercial gain and, often, without permission.

So why are these photographers not liable for appropriation?

They aren't sued because courts generally recognize newsworthiness as a sufficient defense for appropriation.[11] But newsworthiness is not always easy to prove.

A free-lance photographer covering a major football game at Virginia Tech, for example, would probably not be guilty of appropriation for selling to *Sports Illustrated* a photo he took of Michael Vick, who happened to be watching the game on the sidelines. There is little likelihood an appropriation suit would stand even if the magazine ran the photo on its cover. Both the game and Vick's appearance at the game are newsworthy. A person not as well-known as Vick might not be newsworthy and, under some circumstances, might be the subject of a successful

---

[11] No Virginia case exists on the point of the newsworthiness exception to appropriation. *But see* Arrington v. New York Times Co., 434 N.E.2d 1319 (N.Y. 1982); Messenger ex rel. Messenger v. Gruner, 727 N.E.2d 549 (N.Y. 2000).

appropriation suit.[12] In addition, if the photograph of Vick appeared on the cover of a program for a subsequent Virginia Tech football game, and if Vick had not given his permission for the use, both the photographer and the university might be guilty of appropriation.

The primary difference between the two cases is that *Sports Illustrated* is in the business of disseminating information and ideas, an activity protected by the First Amendment. The primary reason the university would sell programs, on the other hand, is to make money, not to disseminate information.

APPROPRIATION	
Tort: The use of a person's name, image or likeness, without permission, for commercial gain.	***Remedy in Virginia:*** Knowing use of a "person's name, portrait or picture in such [appropriation] manner as is forbidden or declared to be unlawful by this chapter, the jury, in its discretion, may award punitive damages." VA. CODE ANN. §8.01-40 (1950).

The importance of this distinction was demonstrated in a 1981 case in the U.S. District Court for the Western District of Virginia. Evangelist Jerry Falwell attempted to halt distribution of the March 1981 issue of *Penthouse* magazine because it contained an interview he had given two free-lance journalists. When his attempt failed, he brought suit

[12] There are no Virginia cases on this point, *but see* Arrington v. New York Times Co., 434 N.E.2d 1319 (N.Y. 1982), *cert. denied* 459 U.S. 1146 (1983).

against *Penthouse* claiming a variety of wrongs, including false light invasion of privacy and appropriation.

A federal court dismissed the false light claim, noting that the cause of action does not exist under Virginia law.[13] The court recognized that the interview was published in *Penthouse* for the purpose of commercial gain, but noted that "everything that appears in a magazine is placed with the intention of increasing sales." To construe the appropriation rule so broadly that it would cover such a case, the court held, would conflict with "important constitutional freedoms, which guarantee the uninhibited dissemination of ideas."[14]

A Richmond judge, however, interpreted the statute just that broadly in March 1998 when he ruled that an appropriation suit based on a novel could go to trial. The parents of two people killed at an Interstate 64 rest stop in September 1989 sued Patricia Cornwell for invasion of privacy, claiming that details in Cornwell's 1992 novel *All That Remains* were based, in part, on autopsies conducted on the bodies of their children. Recognizing that Virginia only allows an invasion of privacy suit when the likeness of a person is used without permission for advertising or trade purposes, Judge Melvin R. Hughes Jr. ruled that the parents could attempt to prove to a jury that the descriptions in the novel were for advertising or trade

---

[13] *Falwell vs. Penthouse Int'l,* 670, 521 F. Supp. 1204, 1206 (W.D. Va. 1981).

[14] *Id.* at 1210. *See also* Falwell v. Flynt, 797 F.2d 1270, 1278 (4th Cir. 1986), *rev'd on other grounds,* 485 U.S. 46 (1988).

purposes.[15] Nine months later, however, Judge Hughes dismissed the privacy claim, ruling that the events in the novel differed from the details of the actual killings and that Cornwell's characters are fictitious.[16]

A real estate firm also claimed to use the name of a celebrity for information rather than advertising purposes, but the Virginia Supreme Court did not buy the claim. In 1991, Hall of Fame football player John Riggins was divorced from Mary Lou Riggins. Later that year, Mrs. Riggins, a real estate broker, placed on the market the house she had acquired as part of the divorce settlement and made the sale known with a flyer that advertised the house as being Riggins' former home. The house was in Northern Virginia where Riggins, a former member of the Washington Redskins football team, was well known. Riggins, who received fees for personal appearances and for lending his name to advertising ventures, sued for appropriation and won more than $53,000 in damages.[17]

The real estate company argued that it should not be required to pay damages for the disclosure of truthful, public information. The identity of Riggins' ownership of the property "is an immutable characteristic" of the property, the company argued,

---

[15] *See* Alan Cooper, *Invasion of Privacy Lawsuit Against Cornwell to Proceed,* RICHMOND TIMES-DISPATCH, Mar. 2, 1998, at B1.

[16] *See Metro In Brief,* WASHINGTON POST, Dec. 16, 1998, at B3.

[17] Town & Country Properties, Inc. v. Riggins, 457 S.E.2d 356, 358-60 (Va. 1995).

and the information was freely available to the public from Fairfax County land records.[18]

The state supreme court disagreed. The flyer was clearly advertising material, the court held, and Riggins' name was used to enhance the probability of ultimate sale of the property. Therefore, the court concluded that the name was used for advertising purposes, as specifically forbidden by state law.[19]

Appropriation, therefore, is not purely an invasion of privacy tort, though it is recognized as such in most states. Regardless of legal distinctions, however, appropriation may be used in Virginia to protect the image or likeness of a person from unauthorized use.

INTRUSION

Intrusion occurs when a place where a person has a reasonable expectation of privacy is physically invaded. The tort has nothing to do with publication. The mere act of intrusion is itself the tort. The invasion occurs because of electronic eavesdropping, the use of high-powered photographic lenses to snoop into a person's back yard, peeping through a bedroom window, or similar activities.

Virginia does not recognize intrusion as an invasion of privacy tort in either statutory or common law, but that doesn't mean Virginia law allows journalists – or anyone else – free access to homes, businesses and other places individuals could ordinarily expect privacy. A bundle of Virginia

---

[18] *Id.* at 361-62.

[19] *Id.* 362-63.

statutes protect privacy in such places. Indeed, Virginia legislators have expressed their attitude toward the significance of the privacy of the home:

> It is hereby declared that the protection and preservation of the home is the keystone of democratic government; that the public health and welfare and the good order of the community require that members of the community enjoy in their homes a feeling of well-being, tranquility, and privacy, and when absent from their homes carry with them the sense of security inherent in the assurance that they may return to the enjoyment of their homes.[20]

That declaration accompanies a state law that prohibits the picketing of any residence or home "in a manner which disrupts or threatens to disrupt any individual's right to tranquility in his home."[21] The law is not necessarily designed to protect a person from physical intrusion, but is certainly aimed at protecting peace of mind. And a law that cuts across both intents – peace of mind and protection from intrusion – might be Virginia's prohibition against the burning of a cross on private property, if the burning is done with an intent to intimidate anyone. Virginia's original cross-burning statute was declared unconstitutional by the U.S. Supreme Court due to statutory construction, but the Court held that a tightly

---

[20] VA. CODE ANN. §18.2-418 (1950).

[21] VA. CODE ANN. § 18.2-419 (1950).

constructed statute banning intimidation through cross-burning would be constitutionally valid.[22]

INTRUSION	
Tort: The physical invasion of a place where a person has a reasonable expectation of privacy.	***Remedy in Virginia:*** Prohibition against picketing residences, "Peeping Tom" statute, trespassing statutes. VA. CODE Ann. § 18.2-419 (1950); VA. CODE ANN. § 18.2-386.1 (1950); VA. CODE ANN. § 18.2-119 (1950).

At least two other statutes also protect individual privacy in a manner related to intrusion. What is often called a "peeping Tom" statute prohibits any person from going onto private property for the purpose of secretly looking into a dwelling. The law applies to both permanent structures – like houses and apartment complexes – and temporary structures – like tents or motor homes. The law does not apply to law enforcement officers conducting criminal investigations. Violators of this law, which does not apply to law enforcement officers conducting criminal

[22] Virginia v. Black, 538 U.S. 343 (2003). In 2001, the cross-burning statute was challenged in the Virginia Supreme Court, which held that the statute was unconstitutional. The U.S. Supreme Court held that although components of Virginia's cross burning statute were constitutional the statute's claim that cross-burning was prima facie evidence of intimidation was unconstitutional. *See* discussion of *Black v. Commonwealth* and *Elliot v. Commonwealth* in Chapter 3.

investigations, are guilty misdemeanors.[23] A second statute prohibits the photographing or filming, without permission, of any person who is partially clothed or nude and who is in a place where the person "would have a reasonable expectation of privacy."[24]

Trespassing laws are among the most common methods of protecting an individual's right to the private enjoyment of home or business. Virginia trespassing laws prohibit a person from going onto or remaining on private property after having been forbidden to do so.[25] The order may be oral or written. Therefore, a person is guilty of a misdemeanor when the person goes onto property that has a sign posted warning people to stay away.

If no sign is visible, a person can presume that permission to enter property has been given and may go upon that property. The person must leave when ordered to do so by the owner or custodian of the property, however. In addition, the Virginia Supreme Court has ruled that trespassing statutes apply to public as well as private property.[26] Specific statutes also make it a crime to enter a school, church or cemetery without permission.[27]

---

[23] VA. CODE ANN. § 18.2-130 (1950).

[24] VA. CODE ANN. § 18.2-386.1 (1950).

[25] VA. CODE ANN. § 18.2-119 (1950).

[26] Johnson et al. v. Commonwealth, 186 S.E.2d 53 (Va. 1972), *cert. denied,* 407 U.S. 925 (1972). The case involved a group of students convicted of trespassing after demonstrating at Madison College, now James Madison University.

[27] VA. CODE ANN. §§ 18.2-125 , 18.2-128 & 18.2-129 (1950).

How do the trespassing statutes apply to journalists and photographers?

Trespassing statutes protect the privacy of individuals only from the actual presence of others. That is, the law allows people who own or control property to keep individuals from going onto that property. The law does not protect the privacy of individuals if their activity may be witnessed from public property.

Therefore, a person is allowed to stand on a public sidewalk and witness any activity occurring on private property. The witness may write about what is seen or heard and, indeed, may photograph anything visible. But, while no Virginia cases speak to the point, the witness is likely to encounter legal problems by using special photographic or sound equipment to record activity on private property that could not be seen or heard from public property. Wire tapping or electronic eavesdropping, of course, are prohibited by both state and federal statutes. The Virginia wire tapping law allows the tape recording of telephone conversations if one party to the conversation is aware that it is being recorded.[28]

Newsworthy events often occur on private property – whether that property is the home of an individual or a shopping mall owned by a conglomerate. When those events occur, journalists may presume that they have a license to enter the property. They may also presume they have a right to record what they see and hear. When ordered to leave the property by its owner or custodian, however, again,

---

[28] VA. CODE ANN. § 19.2-62 (1950).

whether that property is a home or a shopping mall, they are in danger of facing criminal and civil charges if they remain.[29]

The law requires journalists to leave property when ordered. Nothing in the law, however, prohibits journalists or photographers from recording what they can as they leave. If a law enforcement officer orders a photographer to stop taking pictures, however, certain additional statutes may apply. A variety of Virginia laws require citizens to obey orders of law enforcement officers in their attempts to, among other things, preserve the peace.[30] A photographer could conceivably be charged under one of these statutes by an officer who argued that the continued activities of the photographer disrupted the peace.

Conversely, two Virginia statutes give journalists a special privilege of access to emergency scenes, even when other citizens must stay away. The statutes allow members of the press to cross police or fire perimeters to cover fires, accidents or other emergency situations.[31] The statutes explicitly prohibit reporters from obstructing police or emergency personnel and implicitly allow the officers to remain in control of the scene, with the power to

---

[29] *See, e.g.,* Hall v. Commonwealth, 49 S.E.2d 369 (Va. 1948) (upholding the convictions of several Jehovah's Witnesses arrested for trespassing after being told not to hand out pamphlets at Monroe Terrace Apartments in Richmond).

[30] *See, e.g.,* VA. CODE ANN. §18.2-463 (1950) (making it a crime to refuse to help an officer in the execution of his office); VA. CODE ANN. §18.2-464 (1950) (making it a crime to fail to obey an order of a conservator of the peace).

[31] VA. CODE ANN. §§15.2-1714 & 27-15.1 (1950).

order members of the press to leave should their presence cause problems.

Ostensibly, these statutes are at odds with trespassing statutes. What happens when an emergency occurs on private property? Virginia law allows reporters to cross police barricades to cover the events, but also allows the owner of the property to order the journalists to leave.

The Virginia Supreme Court has not been required to decide such a case so there is no way of knowing how these competing rights would be balanced. A good rule of thumb for journalists, however, is to obey law enforcement officers and abide by the law.

INTENTIONAL INFLICTION OF EMOTIONAL DISTRESS

Intentional infliction of emotional distress is a relatively recent tort, as it is applied to the media at any rate. It occurs when someone "by extreme and outrageous conduct intentionally or recklessly causes severe emotional distress to another."[32]

Intentional infliction, therefore, prompts some of the same reactions – outrage, embarrassment, distress – as some of the torts that fall under the broad umbrella generally assigned to invasion of privacy.

False light invasion of privacy, for example, is the publicizing of false material that, while not defamatory, might embarrass or enrage an individual.[33] A false light suit is not brought to recover for a damaged reputation, therefore, but to recover from the

---

[32] RESTATEMENT, *supra* note 2, at § 46.

[33] *Id.* at § 652C.

embarrassment or outrage caused by a publication. An intentional infliction suit may be brought for those same reasons.

Similarly, the publication of private information causes distress because material that should be hidden from public view is suddenly given undue publicity.[34] The suit is brought because of the distress caused by the publication of the private material.

FALSE LIGHT INVASION OF PRIVACY	
Tort: The publicizing of false information that may embarrass or enrage a person.	***Remedy in Virginia:*** Filing suit for the tort of intentional infliction of emotional distress. Insulting words statute. VA. CODE § 18.2-416 (1950).

Since false light and publication of private information torts are not recognized in Virginia, a suit for intentional infliction of emotional distress, depending upon the circumstances, may be substituted, even though intentional infliction is synonymous with neither of them. In addition, the burden of proof for an intentional infliction suit does not match that of any invasion of privacy torts. All four torts require some degree of outrageousness, however, so substitution is not an unlikely prospect.

In Virginia, a plaintiff in an intentional infliction suit must meet a four-point burden of proof.[35] The plaintiff must prove:

(1) that the conduct on the part of the defendant was intentional or reckless;

---

[34] *Id.* at § 652D.

[35] Womack v. Eldridge, 210 S.E.2d 145, 148 (1974).

(2) that the conduct offends generally accepted standards of decency or morality;

(3) that the conduct caused emotional distress, and

(4) that the emotional distress was severe.

In addition, a plaintiff who is a public figure or a public official must prove that the publication was made with actual malice, that is, with knowledge of falsity or with reckless disregard for the truth.[36] The severity of distress is frequently an issue that is much debated at trial. Under Virginia law, the distress required should be "so severe that no reasonable person could be expected to endure it."[37] Evidence of this distress includes hospitalizations, physical illness, lost wages and similar factors.[38] It is important to note that no one manifestation of distress is dispositive of severity. Applying Virginia law, a federal trial court in 2014 held that "injury, damage, humiliation, inconvenience, embarrassment, litigation expense, denial of employment, severe mental anguish, attorneys' fees, and pain" did not have the required level of severity of distress needed for a successful intentional infliction of emotional distress suit.[39]

The *Restatement of Torts* summarizes the intentional infliction test this way:

---

[36] Hustler Magazine v. Falwell, 485 U.S. 46, 56 (1988).

[37] Russo v. White, 400 S.E.2d 160, 163 (Va. 1991).

[38] *See* Crittendon v. Arai Americas, Inc. No. 2:13-CV-567, 2014 WL 31490 (E.D. Va. Jan. 3, 2014).

[39] *Id.* at * 5.

> Liability has been found only where the conduct has been so outrageous in character, and so extreme in degree, as to go beyond all possible bounds of decency, and to be regarded as atrocious, and utterly intolerable in a civilized community. Generally, the case is one in which the recitation of the facts to an average member of the community would arouse his resentment against the actor, and lead him to exclaim, "Outrageous!"[40]

In cases involving the media, intentional infliction has been found when a magazine published a sexually explicit classified advertisement giving the name and address of a woman who did not place the ad,[41] when a team physician wrongly reported that a pro football player had a fatal disease,[42] when a photographer obsessively followed Jacqueline Kennedy Onassis and her children,[43] when a television crew filmed a CEO's family,[44] and when a television news team followed paramedics into a private home

---

[40] RESTATEMENT, *supra* note 2, at §46, comment d.

[41] Vesco v. New Way Enter., Ltd., 60 Cal. App. 3d 582 (1976).

[42] Chuy v. Philadelphia Eagles Football Club, 431 F. Supp. 254 (E.D. Pa. 1977).

[43] Galella v. Onassis, 487 F.2d 986 (2d Cir. 1973).

[44] Wolfson v. Lewis et al., 924 F.Supp. 1413 (E.D. Pa. 1996).

and filmed unsuccessful efforts to resuscitate a heart-attack victim.[45]

There was no outrageous conduct, however, in the publication of the name and address of the sole witness to an armed robbery and murder,[46] in the publication of names listed in a report on organized crime,[47] in the publication of a story and photographs about children suffocating in a discarded refrigerator,[48] or in the publication of the identity and photograph of an undercover narcotics officer.[49]

PUBLICATION OF PRIVATE INFORMATION	
Tort: The widespread dissemination of private information.	***Remedy in Virginia:*** None

One of the best examples of intentional infliction of emotional distress is *Hustler Magazine v. Falwell,*[50] which was tried in U.S. District Court in Roanoke and eventually made its way to the U.S. Supreme Court.

---

[45] Miller v. Nat'l Broad. Co., 187 Cal. App. 3d 1463 (1986).

[46] Hood v. Naeter Bros. Publ'g Co., 562 S.W.2d 770 (Mo. App. 1978).

[47] Kilgore v. Younger, 640 P.2d 793 (Cal. 1982).

[48] Costlow v. Cusimano, 34 A.D.2d 196 (N.Y. App. Div. 1970).

[49] Ross v. Burns, 612 F.2d 271 (6th Cir. 1980).

[50] At the circuit court level the case was Falwell v. Flynt, 797 F.2d 1270 (4th Cir. 1986).

Hustler published a parody of a Campari Liquor advertisement in which the Rev. Jerry Falwell was portrayed as saying that his first sexual experience was a drunken encounter with his mother in an outhouse. The Campari Liquor campaign involved celebrities describing their first experiences drinking the liquor. Double entendre, however, implied that the celebrities were describing their first sexual encounters.

Larry Flynt, the publisher of *Hustler,* testified at trial that one purpose of the parody was to portray Falwell as a liar, glutton and hypocrite and to assassinate his integrity.[51] Falwell testified that he had never been as angry or as deeply wounded by any publication. He testified that he had never physically attacked anyone, but, when he saw the publication, "I really think that at that moment if Larry Flynt had been nearby I might have physically reacted."[52]

The jury found that the parody was published with intent to cause severe emotional distress and that it did, indeed, cause such distress.

The U.S. Supreme Court overturned the verdict on other grounds. Though not disturbing the finding that the publication was outrageous or that Falwell had suffered severe emotional distress, the Court held that a public figure must prove actual malice in order to win a suit for intentional infliction of emotional distress.[53] The Court's ruling also indicated that there

---

[51] *Falwell,* 797 F.2d at 1273.

[52] *Id.* at 1276.

[53] *Hustler v. Falwell,* 485 U.S. 46, 56 (1988). Actual malice, which is defined as knowledge of falsity or reckless

must be an effort on the part of the plaintiff to pass off as the truth material that is false, and, since the parody could not be reasonably construed as being true, there could be no liability.[54]

In addition, in its 2010-11 term, the Supreme Court, in all likelihood, eliminated intentional infliction of emotional distress as a speech-based tort. That is, the tort is only viable if it involves actions. The Court has made it clear that neither publications – writings, broadcasts, Web pages – nor picketing may be the basis for successful intentional infliction suits.

The ruling came in *Snyder v. Phelps*,[55] a case in which the father of a dead Marine claimed that the picketing by Westboro Baptist Church and a posting on the church's Web site that attacked the dead man and his family had caused him severe emotional distress and that the activity of the church was both intentional and outrageous.[56] A district court agreed, but the U.S. Supreme Court, giving short shrift to the claims by the father, held that the fact that the picketing occurred on public property outweighed any emotional distress it may have caused. The court's rationale was that the Westboro Baptist Church's protests focused on homosexuality, the Roman Catholic Church abuse scandal, 9/11 attacks, and gays in the military, which were all matters of public concern. This category of speech is highly protected

---

disregard for the truth, *New York Times Co. v. Sullivan*, 376 U.S. 254, 271 (1964), is discussed in detail in Chapter 5.

[54] *Id.* at 57.

[55] 562 U.S. 443 (2011).

[56] *Id.* at 451.

under the First Amendment. Because of this, the court held that the jury verdict finding that the protests caused emotional distress had to be overturned given the First Amendment protection of the content of the protests. The Court did not consider the Web posting.

It is important to note that plaintiffs of intentional infliction of emotional distress need not be well-known celebrities like Falwell or involve widely publicized events such as the Westboro Baptist Church's protests. In 2007, Botetourt County farmer Andrew Marsinko, a member of American Poultry Exhibitor's Hall of Frame, brought a $7.5 million lawsuit against a photographer, a greeting card company, and a digital image provider for the sale and use of his image without his express permission. The card featured a photo of Marsinko holding his prize groose at the 1995 Virginia State Fair. The card caption read, "Since it's your birthday would you rather be spanked—or goosed?" Marsinko stated that he did not know about the card until 2006 when he attended an auction in Mount Hope, Ohio. During that event, Marsinko claimed he was regularly ridiculed because of his image on the card. This ridicule and teasing continued at other events Marsinko attended in Illinois, Delaware, Maryland and Virginia. As a result, Marsinko filed suit in Roanoke County Circuit Court for defamation, unauthorized use of picture, conspiracy, attempted conspiracy, and intentional or reckless infliction of emotional distress.[57] The lawsuit was settled out of court.

---

[57] Marsinko v. Burwell et al., No. CL07001070-00 (Roanoke Circuit, Filed Sep. 12, 2007); Marsinko v. Burwell et al., 2008 Va. Cir. LEXIS 125 (Cir. Ct. 2008) (Roanoke County).

INSULTING OR ABUSIVE LANGUAGE

As previously indicated, intentional infliction of emotional distress might be used as a substitute for various invasion of privacy torts, including false light invasion of privacy. Virginia's insulting words and abusive language statutes may be used in the same way.

False light invasion of privacy occurs when false material, which is often insulting, is published about an individual. An insulting words or abusive language suit may be brought when something false and insulting is said *to* a person.

The chapter on libel points out that a suit for insulting words is treated "precisely as an action for slander or libel for words actionable per se, with one exception, namely, no publication is necessary."[58] The state supreme court, however, has also indicated that the insulting words statute continues to provide the means for a cause of action when non-defamatory words "tend to violence and breach of peace," that is, when they are fighting words.[59] Words are actionable, therefore, if they would tend to cause an immediate violent response or a breach of the peace.[60] It is not necessary for those words to be published or to be defamatory.

Similarly, under Virginia law a person may not use abusive language to another in public. The law

---

[58] Carwile v. Richmond Newspapers, 82 S.E.2d 588, 591 (Va. 1954).

[59] Allen & Rocks, Inc. v. Dowell, 477 S.E.2d 741 (Va. 1996).

[60] VA. CODE ANN. § 8.01-45 (1950).

provides that a person may not "in the presence or hearing of another, curse or abuse such other person, or use any violent abusive language to such person concerning himself or any of his relations."[61] The statute has been held to be constitutional by the Virginia Court of Appeals.[62] Courts, however, have not enunciated a definition of what words would constitute abuse.[63]

---

[61] VA. CODE ANN. § 18.2-416 (1950).

[62] Perkins v. Commonwealth, 402 S.E.2d 229 (Va. App. 1991).

[63] *See* Thompson v. Town of Port Royal et al., No. CIV.A. 5:98CV00083, 2000 WL 329237 (W.D. Va. 2000); Stinson v. McCarthy 25 Va. Cir. 407 (Cir. Ct. 1991) (Fairfax County).

7. ACCESS TO PUBLIC MEETINGS AND OFFICIAL DOCUMENTS

The Virginia General Assembly adopted the state's Freedom of Information Act in 1968 to ensure "the people of the Commonwealth ready access to public records in the custody of a public body or its officers and employees and free entry to meetings of public bodies wherein the business of the people is being conducted." That's because, legislators wrote, "The affairs of government are not intended to be conducted in an atmosphere of secrecy since at all times the public is to be the beneficiary of any action taken at any level of government."[1]

To help ensure openness, then, the law is to be "liberally construed to promote an increased awareness by all persons of governmental activities and afford every opportunity to citizens to witness the operations of government." And any exceptions or exemptions "shall be narrowly construed and no record shall be withheld or meeting closed to the public unless specifically made exempt" by the law.[2]

The law, then, requires that citizens be allowed access to records and documents related to the conduct of public business and to meetings of official bodies. The law is not a press law, but a citizen's law, premised on the philosophy that citizens have a right to know how their business is being conducted. For that

---

[1] VA. CODE ANN. § 2.2-3700(B) (1950).

[2] *Id.*

reason, there are no prerequisites for access; a citizen has a right to see official records or attend public meetings without tendering reasons.

In addition, since the law is to be liberally construed and exceptions are to be narrowly construed, legal interpretations are to weigh in favor of citizens.

Access is not absolute, however. Some records may be kept from public scrutiny, some business may be conducted behind closed doors, and the act does not apply to some agencies – the Virginia Parole Board, the Virginia State Crime Commission, petit juries, grand juries and, significantly, to informal meetings of members of the Virginia General Assembly.

In addition, lawmakers fiddle with the Freedom of Information Act during every session of the general assembly. The last attempt to streamline the entire act came in 1999, when a number of changes were made. The act remains cumbersome, however, and some of its restrictions border on absurdity. For example, the records portion of the act allows the Department of Game and Inland Fisheries to keep secret the subscription list for its magazine *Virginia Wildlife*. The exemption was added when a constituent complained to her legislator that she didn't want her name disseminated to companies that might use it for solicitations. The legislator was able to get the exemption added to the act.[3]

---

[3] Del. Jay DeBoer, Address: Open Government: What Part Do Executive Sessions Play?, at a public forum sponsored by the League of Women Voters of Montgomery County (Mar. 23, 1998). *See also* VA. CODE ANN. § 2.1-3705.7(13) (1950).

The Freedom of Information Act, then, is becoming increasingly complex as lawmakers attach provisos, limitations and exceptions. In addition, rulings by the Virginia Supreme Court, which has never indicated genuine concern for the public's right to know, have weakened the act.

While the FOIA remains cumbersome, the general assembly made a genuine effort to make it more workable when, in 2000, it established the Freedom of Information Advisory Council. The purpose of the twelve-member council is to "encourage and facilitate compliance with the Freedom of Information Act" by issuing advisory opinions, conducting training sessions and publishing educational materials.[4] Maria Everett, an attorney with the Division of Legislative Services, was named executive director of the council.[5]

The Virginia Coalition for Open Government also works to ensure open government. The non-profit organization was established in 1996 to enhance the flow of information to citizens in the commonwealth. It monitors access issues and lobbies for increased access to the workings of government.[6]

Official Records

---

4 Va. Code Ann. §§ 2.1-346.2 & 2.1-346.3 (1950).

5 The council's advisory opinions, and other information, are posted on the council's Web page, http://dls.state.va.us/foiacouncil.htm.

6 The Web page for the Virginia Coalition for Open Government is http://opengovva.org/.

The Virginia Freedom of Information Act provides that any citizen of the commonwealth shall be permitted to inspect and copy official records "during the regular office hours of the custodian of such records." The law also allows access by representatives of newspapers and magazines that circulate in the state and by representatives of radio and television stations that broadcast into the state.[7] Official records are defined as

> [A]ll writings and recordings that consist of letters, words or numbers, or their equivalent, set down by handwriting, typewriting, printing, photostatting, photography, magnetic impulse, optical or magneto-optical form, mechanical or electronic recording or other form of data compilation, however stored, and regardless of physical form or characteristics, prepared or owned by, or in the possession of a public body or its officers, employees or agents in the transaction of public business. Records that are not prepared for or used in the transaction of public business are not public records.[8]

The section has been construed to include items as varied as a jail log,[9] mug shots of criminal

---

[7] Official records are covered in VA. CODE ANN. § 2.2.3704 (1950); criminal records are covered in VA. CODE ANN. § 2.2.3706 (1950).

[8] VA. CODE ANN. § 2.2-3701 (1950).

[9] 1987-88 Rep. A.G. 37, 1983-84 Rep. A.G. 446, 1980-81 Rep. A.G. 391, 1976-77 Rep. A.G. 250, 1974-75 Rep. A.G.

suspects,[10] and a public school principal's handwritten notes on a person suspected of stealing school property.[11] Medical information on a jail inmate,[12] records of the governor's long-distance telephone calls[13] and tape recordings of 911 emergency telephone calls,[14] on the other hand, lie outside the reach of the act.

Also covered by the act is information held in computer databases maintained by government entities. As of July 1, 1997, every government agency that stored information in computer databases has been required to maintain indexes of documents in those databases. As a practical matter, however, most government agencies don't maintain these indexes. The law also provides that the indexes themselves are public records.

The law only grants mandatory access to records by Virginia residents, a provision that was upheld as constitutional by the U.S. Supreme Court in 2013. In *McBurney v. Young,* Mark J. McBurney, a Rhode Island resident who was involved in a child-support dispute with his former wife, a resident of

---

583. Attorney general's opinions represent an interpretation of the law by the commonwealth's chief law enforcement officer, but they are not binding.

[10] 1990 Rep. A.G. 9. But VA. CODE ANN. § 2.3-3706(1)(b) allows photographs of persons who have been arrested to be withheld if release would jeopardize criminal investigations.

[11] 1983-84 Rep. A.G. 437.

[12] 1987-88 Rep. A.G. 33.

[13] Taylor v. Worrell Enterprises, Inc., 409 S.E.2d 136 (Va. 1991).

[14] Tull v. Brown, 494 S.E.2d 855 (Va. 1998).

Virginia, sought all documents related to his family held by the state Division of Child Support Enforcement. And Roger W. Hurlbert, California resident who was a provider of real estate tax information, sought real estate tax records from Henrico County. Both requests were denied because of the citizenship requirement. They sought the records under the Privileges and Immunities Clause and the dormant Commerce Clause of the U.S. Constitution.[15]

The Court found no violation of either clause in the denial.[16] Megan Rhyne, executive director of the Virginia Coalition for Open Government, expressed disappointment at the decision and said that a stronger case would probably be made on the issue of access to records held by public bodies.[17]

Law Enforcement Documents

Records held by law enforcement agencies have probably caused more controversy in Virginia than any other. The act requires that "criminal incident information relating to felony offenses" be released. The information may be withheld temporarily, however, if the release is likely to jeopardize an ongoing investigation, jeopardize the safety of an individual, cause a suspect to flee or cause the destruction of evidence.[18] Criminal incident information is defined as general information about criminal activity, including the date and location of the

---

[15] 133 S.Ct. 1709, 1713-14 (2013).

[16] *Id.* at 1713.

[17] Interview with Megan Rhyne, June 2013.

[18] VA. CODE ANN. § 2.2.3706(1)(a) (1950).

crime, identity of the investigating officer and a description of injuries or property loss.

The act does not provide for the release of criminal incident information regarding misdemeanors, however, and it does not provide for the release of criminal incident reports, those documents used by law enforcement agencies to record incidents under investigation.

In addition, the law allows specific types of records to be withheld:

- complaints, memoranda, correspondence and evidence related to a criminal investigation or prosecution;
- photographs of persons arrested, unless the release of the photograph will not jeopardize the investigation;
- reports submitted in confidence;
- records that would identify anonymous sources;
- records related to neighborhood watch programs;
- records of prison inmates.

The law, therefore, leaves in the hands of law enforcement agencies, considerable discretion as to the types of information to be released and when that information will be released. Since the law does not require access to criminal incident reports, law enforcement agencies can arbitrarily withhold information or can require citizens to see specific officers – the police chief or a public relations officer, for example – who may purposefully be unavailable.

In addition, when disputes arise over whether a document should be released, courts often rule in favor of government agencies. In 1998, for example, the Virginia Supreme Court denied access to a tape recording of a 911 emergency telephone call, even though a transcript of the recording had been made available to the media.[19] The Surry County Circuit Court had ruled that the tape was not an official document under the Freedom of Information Act. The Virginia Supreme Court disagreed, holding that the tape recording is an official record, but that it is exempt from disclosure as part of "noncriminal incidents records."[20]

In addition, in 2015, the court allowed the withholding of a record in a criminal investigation file even though the case had been closed. Benjamin B. Fitzgerald sought what purported to be a suicide note left by Charles D. Riechers, a senior United States Air Force Official working in the Pentagon.[21] An investigation by Loudon County officials determined Riechers' death to be a suicide and closed the case. Fitzgerald argued that the criminal investigative file "lost its character as such when the file was closed." Though some records related to the investigation were released to Fitzgerald, the suicide note was not. The

---

[19] Tull v. Brown, 494 S.E.2d 855 (1998).

[20] *Id.* 494 S.E.2d at 855. Certain non-criminal incident records are exempt from disclosure under VA. CODE ANN. § 2.2-3706(3)(B). Records related to "noncriminal occurrences of general interest to law-enforcement agencies," including missing persons, lost and found reports, suicides and accidental deaths are exempt from disclosure under VA. CODE ANN. § 15.2-1722 (1950).

[21] Fitzgerald v. Loudon County Sheriff's Office, 771 S.E.2d 858, 859 (Va. 2015).

court, finding that release of such documents was discretionary and holding that nothing in the statute supported Fitzgerald's argument, allowed Loudon County officials to withhold the note.[22]

Exemptions

The Freedom of Information Act recognizes that certain documents may be withheld from public view for the sake of privacy or for efficient government operation. In addition to the law enforcement documents described previously, some 130 exemptions cover documents containing information relating to topics as varied as fisheries, public libraries, and the Virginia State Lottery.[23]

The exemptions are categorized this way:[24]

- Exclusions of general application to public bodies (13 exemptions), including personnel records that identify individuals, written advice from legal counsel, and records recorded in or compiled for closed sessions.
- Records relating to public safety (16 exemptions), including records held by rape crisis centers identifying victims, plans and information preventing or responding to terrorist activity or cyber attacks, school safety audits, and certain hospital records.[25]

---

[22] *Id.* at 861.

[23] VA. CODE ANN. § 2.1-342.01 (1950).

[24] VA. CODE ANN. § 2.2-3705.1 (1950).

[25] VA. CODE ANN. § 2.2-3705.3 (1950).

- Records related to administrative investigations (13 exemptions), including internal investigations by a number of state agencies or the attorney general.[26]
- Educational records (eight exemptions), including scholastic records, recommendations related to admission or awards, proprietary information held by certain universities, and fundraising records.[27]
- Health and social services records (19 exemptions), including medical records, applications for licensing by the Department of Health Professions, and investigative notes held by the Department of Social Services.[28]
- Proprietary records and trade secrets (27 exemptions) including a number of kinds of financial reports, fisheries data and similar records.[29]
- Records held by specific public bodies (34 exemptions), including various tax records, working papers of the governor, lieutenant governor, attorney general, members of the General Assembly and other bodies; library records; records listing subscribers to *Virginia Wildlife* magazine; records of the Judicial Inquiry and Review Committee; names and contact information of individual who correspond with public bodies.[30]

---

[26] VA. CODE ANN. § 2.2-3705.2 (1950).

[27] VA. CODE ANN. § 2.2-3705.4 (1950).

[28] VA. CODE ANN. § 2.2-3705.5 (1950).

[29] VA. CODE ANN. § 2.2-3705.6 (1950).

[30] VA. CODE ANN. § 2.2-3705.7 (1950). The last of these exemptions does not go into effect until July 1, 2018.

The law does not require all these records be withheld from disclosure. In most cases, the custodian of the record may release the documents – the law simply allows the custodian to withhold it. In almost all cases, however, documents will be withheld if the law so-allows.

Often, the exemptions to disclosure are easy to apply. Sometimes, however, courts are called upon to interpret the law to determine whether documents and information should be released. And sometimes those interpretations border on the absurd. In 1996, for example, the Virginia Supreme Court held that the results of a student government elections at a high school constituted scholastic records and, therefore, that a principal was justified in withholding the information.[31] Following elections at Centreville High School in Fairfax County, the editor of the school's student newspaper asked for a complete tally of the votes. The request was denied because, school officials said, the vote totals would embarrass students who did not win seats in the elections. The student sued and, in *Wall v. Fairfax County School Board,* the state supreme court, assuming that the vote total is an official record, said the information could be withheld as scholastic records.[32]

A year later the Virginia Senate adopted a bill amending the FOIA so that information so obviously public could not be withheld by school officials, but the bill did not pass the house of delegates.

---

[31] Wall v. Fairfax Cty. Sch. Bd., 475 S.E.2d 803 (1996).

[32] *Id.* at 805.

The Virginia Supreme Court has also held that the governor was not required under the Freedom of Information Act to release documents revealing long distance telephone calls he had made. A requirement for the governor to release information about such phone calls, the court held, would unreasonably impair his ability to perform his duties as chief executive. The court determined, therefore, that the general assembly had not intended to require mandatory disclosure of the records.[33]

Procedures for Access

A citizen is not required to state a reason for seeing a specific document; the citizen need only ask to see the document. The citizen, therefore, must know the identity of the custodian of the specific record being sought. The clerk of circuit court, for example, is responsible for the court records; the sheriff is responsible for jail records; the superintendent of schools is responsible for school budgeting documents.

The duty to get the records request to the correct agency is not fully in the hands of a citizen, however. If a public body does not possess a record but the custodian knows that the record is in the hands of another agency, the law requires that the response from the custodian to the person requesting the record must include contact information for the other public body.[34] In addition, since the act grants the right of access to citizens, the custodian of the records may

---

[33] Taylor v. Worrell Enterprises, Inc., 409 S.E.2d 136, 139-40 (Va. 1991).

[34] VA. CODE ANN. § 2.2-3704(B)(3) (1950).

legally refuse to produce a record for a person who is not a citizen of the commonwealth unless that person represents a news organization that circulates or broadcasts into the commonwealth.

When a request is made for access to an official document, the custodian, within five working days, must respond by:

- providing the record;
- refusing to provide the record and explaining in writing which exemption applies;
- providing the record with certain portions deleted and explaining in writing which exemption applies to the deleted portions; or,
- explaining that the record cannot be provided within the five-day deadline. The agency then has an additional seven days in which to provide the record or explain why it is exempt from the provisions of the act.

Failure to respond to a request for access to an official record is deemed a denial of the record and is a violation of the law, as a case involving the Norfolk Airport Authority demonstrates. John H. Fenter sought information from the airport authority related to signs posted indicating that the authority had the right to search all vehicles on its property. The authority responded to Fenter's FOIA request indicating that it was seeking additional information about what it could release from the Transportation Security Administration and legal counsel.[35] The court held

---

[35] Fenter v. Norfolk Airport Auth., 649 S.E.2d 704, 706-07 (Va. 2007).

that these responses did not meet the requirements of FOIA and was, therefore, a violation of the act. It also held that Fenter could recover costs and attorney's fees from the authority.[36]

If a request is for an unusually large number of records or if there are other extenuating circumstances, a public agency may petition the court for additional time in which to provide the records requested.

In addition, the agency may charge reasonable fees for "accessing, duplicating, supplying or searching for the required records." The law specifies, however, that the charges shall not exceed the actual cost to a public body for supplying the records. Indeed, the state attorney general has said it is unreasonable to charge a newspaper for the salary of an employee whose sole task it was to watch a reporter inspect the minutes of a town council meeting.[37] The agency may also seek advance payment if it determines that the cost of producing the record will be more than $200.

The Virginia Supreme Court has also interpreted this part of the law to allow fees for the time necessary to determine whether records may be withheld from disclosure: "[T]he ordinary meaning of 'searching' in this statutory provision permits a public body to charge a reasonable fee for exclusion review."[38]

Finally, the law specifies that no public agency is required to create or prepare documents for citizens

---

[36] *Id.* at 709.

[37] 1989 Rep. A.G. 12.

[38] American Tradition Inst. et al. v. Rector and Visitors of the University of Virginia, 756 S.E.2d 435, 442 (Va. 2014).

if those documents do not already exist. The purpose of the act is to provide public access to existing documents, not to require agencies to create documents. The provision that an agency not be required to create a document has been enforced even in the face of a violation of the law. In *Hale v. Washington County School Board,* the Virginia Supreme Court ruled that a closed session held by the board was invalid, but did not require the board to provide a written summary of the discussion that occurred during that invalid meeting.[39]

The provision that agencies not be required to create a document was used by the state supreme court to allow the denial of access to DNA material. Newspapers, including Virginia papers, sought access to DNA material related to the conviction of Roger Keith Coleman in 1982 for the rape and murder of Wanda McCoy. DNA testing was not available at Coleman's trial, and the newspapers wanted the material in order to have it tested.[40]

The court found, "What the newspapers seek to do in this case is expand the definition of 'access' to include the right to conduct independent testing of evidence in criminal proceedings." In doing so, "[T]he newspapers seek 'access' to something that does not exist, namely, new evidence in the form of new test results." There is no case law to support such "a novel extension of the concept of access." The definition of access "does not include the right of the public at large

---

[39] 400 S.E.2d 175, 177-78 (1991).

[40] Globe Newspaper Co. v. Commonwealth, 570 S.E.2d 809 (Va. 2002).

or the press to subject evidence in a criminal case to testing."[41] In addition, "Clearly, the biological material recovered on swabs from the vagina of the victim does not meet the test of a 'public record.' Even if it did, the VFOIA allows for inspection and copying, not testing."[42]

PUBLIC MEETINGS

The Virginia Freedom of Information Act provides that all meetings of public bodies, including work sessions in which no votes are expected, shall be held in public, and that notice of the time, date and place of the meetings shall be furnished to anyone seeking that information. In addition, the law provides that anyone may photograph, film or record the meetings, but that the public body may adopt rules governing the placement of equipment.[43]

A meeting is defined in the law as any gathering of a quorum or three members of a public body, whichever constitutes fewer people. The law notes, however, that gatherings of two or more members of a public body at a function not intended for the discussion or transaction of public business are not illegal.[44] The Virginia Attorney General has said that social functions do not fall within the purview of the act if there is no evidence that the functions were

---

[41] *Id.* at 812.

[42] *Id.* at 813.

[43] Public meetings are covered in VA. CODE ANN. §§ 2.2-3707 – 2.2-3712 (1950).

[44] VA. CODE ANN. § 2.2-3701 (1950).

prearranged with the purpose of discussing or transacting business.[45]

"Public body" is defined as:

> [A]ny legislative body, authority, board, bureau, commission, district or agency of the Commonwealth or of any political subdivision of the Commonwealth, including cities, towns and counties; municipal council, governing bodies of counties, school boards and planning commissions; boards of visitors of state institutions of higher education; and other organizations, corporations or agencies in the Commonwealth, supported wholly or principally by public funds.[46]

The definition, therefore, is wide-ranging. It includes committees and subcommittees of public bodies. Indeed, a circuit court judge has held that a meeting of two members of a board of supervisors was a meeting under the law when those two members constituted the board's finance committee.[47] The state attorney general has also construed the definition to include a student senate meeting at a public university.[48]

---

[45] 1982-83 Rep. A.G. 721

[46] VA. CODE ANN. §2.2-3701 (1950).

[47] Shenandoah Publ'g House, Inc. v. Shenandoah Cty. Bd. of Supervisors, 22 Med. L. Rptr. (BNA) 1177 (Shenandoah Circuit 1993).

[48] 1982-83 Rep. A.G. 440.

The law also prohibits meetings by use of electronic communications unless members of the public are provided with access to the meeting and the ability to hear the business being conducted.[49]

A political dispute in Fredericksburg following the election of new city council members in 2002 raised a passel of issues regarding the meetings provisions of the FOIA. After their election, but before they were sworn into office, Thomas P. Fortune, William C. Withers Jr. and Matthew J. Kelly began exchanging emails and meeting with Mayor William M. Beck and vice-mayor W. Scott Howson III. Political opponents of the group – Gordon Shelton, Anthony Jenkins and Patrick J. Timpone – filed a lawsuit claiming that the emails and meetings violated the state FOIA. The specific claims were that the law was violated because the email communications constituted meetings under the law for which notice was not given, and that meetings between members of council and members-elect constituted meetings under the law and, therefore, were illegal because of the absence of notice.[50]

The Virginia Supreme Court held that the FOIA applies to members of governing bodies, so it was not illegal for non-council members – even if they are members-elect – meet with members.[51] The court also held that email communications are not considered meetings under the law. While the emails are clearly covered by the records portion of the law, the court

---

[49] VA. CODE ANN. §. 2.2-3708 (1950).

[50] Beck v. Shelton, 593 S.E.2d 195, 196-97 (Va. 2004).

[51] *Id.* at 197-98.

held, unless the electronic communications occur in chat rooms, by instant messaging or similar real-time formats, they do not fit the definition of "meetings" under FOIA.[52]

Finally, in a related matter, three members of the Fredericksburg City Council met at the intersection of two streets in the city as a result of phone calls from residents who were concerned that there was no stop sign at the intersection. The council members were contacted by different residents, and about 20 residents were present when the council members arrived. The court held that the gathering was not a meeting under the law. Calling upon the section of the FOIA that reports that the law "shall not be construed to discourage the free discussion of government officials or employees of public matters with the citizens of the commonwealth," the court found that the gathering was not a "meeting" for purposes of FOIA.[53]

Closed Sessions: Topics for Discussion

The law allows public bodies to hold closed sessions for a variety of reasons, from matters related to the state lottery, to consideration of honorary degrees to matters related to gifts, bequests or grants to the Virginia Museum of Fine Arts or the Science Museum of Virginia.[54]

---

[52] *Id.* at 198-201. *See also* Hill v. Fairfax Cty. Sch. Bd., 727 S.E.2d 75 (Va. 2012).

[53] *Id.* at 200-01.

[54] Closed sessions are covered in VA. CODE ANN. §§ 2.2-3711 – 2.2-3712 (1950). In 2000, the Virginia General Assembly rewrote the Freedom of Information Act, changing the name of

Closed sessions may be held for the purposes of discussion only; no action may be taken in closed sessions. The law does not require public bodies to discuss matters in closed sessions, but allows such sessions to be held if matters fall within one of 47 categories. Some of the most common topics for discussion in closed session are:

- personnel matters, including discussions involving the hiring, firing, discipline, promotion and assignment of public employees;
- consideration of the admission or disciplining of students;
- discussions necessary to protect the privacy of individuals in personal matters not related to public business;
- discussions concerning the acquisition, sale or use of real property; discussions of a prospective business or industry locating within a community, if there has been no previous announcement;
- meetings with attorneys to receive legal advice;
- discussions of tests or examinations; consideration of honorary degrees or special awards;
- discussions of gifts, bequests and fund-raising for state colleges and universities, the Virginia Museum of Fine Arts and the Science Museum of Virginia;
- discussion by the governor and any economic advisory board reviewing forecasts of economic activity;
- discussion of lottery game information and studies;

---

that portion of a meeting held outside public view from "executive session" to "closed session."

- various information related to local crime commissions, corrections resources boards and the Board of Corrections;
- discussion of plans to protect the public safety as it relates to terrorist activity.

Closed Sessions: Legal Requirements & Limits

For a closed session to be legal, certain requirements must be met before, during and after the session.

First, a board may go into closed session only upon a majority vote in open session. The specific purpose of the session is to be stated, reasonably identifying the substance of the matters to be discussed, including a specific reference to the section of the act under which the topic falls. The Virginia Supreme Court has ruled that the topic to be discussed must be specifically identified, but that the body is not required to disclose the topic in detail. "To do so," the court ruled, "would tend to defeat the very confidentiality that the exemption safeguards."[55]

Following the closed session, the board must reconvene in open session, and each member of the board must certify "to the best of that member's knowledge" that the board, while in closed session, discussed only matters the law allows to be discussed in such a session and only those matters identified in the motion by which closed session was convened. The certification must take place with a roll call of the members. The law provides that any member of the

---

[55] Marsh v. Richmond Newspapers, Inc., 288 S.E.2d 415, 420 (Va. 1982).

board who cannot certify is required to indicate "the substance of the departure that, in his judgment, has taken place."

The certification section of the act, which was added in 1989, has caused considerable controversy. Some public officials are offended, claiming that the act presumes that they will attempt to circumvent the law by using closed sessions to discuss any matters they so choose. Indeed, one member of the Montgomery County School Board refused to adhere to the certification requirement, claiming his right not to incriminate himself under the Fifth Amendment to the U.S. Constitution.

It is important to note, that nothing in the FOIA prohibits participants in closed sessions from discussing what transpired during those sessions. While political or ethical considerations may come into play in such situations, the law does not.

Finally, no action taken in closed session is valid. According to the law, any action taken by a public body, even actions on matters discussed in private, must be taken in open session. In addition, all actions must be taken by a public vote – members of public bodies are not allowed to vote on any issues by means of secret ballot.

Evasion and Enforcement of the Law

A Freedom of Information Act is only as good as the efforts of citizens to enforce it and as those in government administering it. Over the years public bodies have tried time and again to evade the provisions of the law. Some of these efforts have resulted in amendments to the act.

The Roanoke City School Board, for example, in the early 1980s began holding discussions of school business by means of conference telephone calls. The Virginia Attorney General issued an opinion stating that the calls constituted "meetings" and, therefore, violated the Freedom of Information Act.[56] The state supreme court, however, ruled that the conference calls were not "meetings" for purposes of the act and, therefore, were legal.[57]

The General Assembly responded by amending the act in 1989, specifically outlawing conference calls, unless the times of the calls are announced and access is available for those who want to listen.

The General Assembly, however, has also left a loophole in the law that became apparent in 1991. The law requires public bodies to announce the time and place of informal as well as formal meetings. The General Assembly is exempt from that provision of the act, however. Because of the exemption, Richmond Circuit Judge Randall Johnson ruled that the Senate Finance Committee was not in violation of the law when it held a meeting at a private hunting lodge during the Christmas holidays in 1990.[58] The Virginia chapter of the American Civil Liberties Union brought suit seeking to open such meetings to the public.

---

[56] 1982-83 Rep. A.G. 446.

[57] Roanoke Sch. Bd. v. Times-World Corp., 307 S.E.2d 256 (Va. 1983). The parameters on the use of conference calls are delineated in section 2.2-3708 of the law.

[58] American Civil Liberties Union of Virginia v. Andrews, Case No. HB-342-4 (Richmond Cir. 1991), slip opinion.

Johnson, however, held that the meeting was obviously informal, even though staff members made a presentation and distributed material related to the state budget. Because the meeting was informal, the committee, as part of the general assembly, was not required to give public notice and there was no violation of the act, Johnson ruled.[59] The ACLU decided not to appeal the case because, ACLU attorney David P. Baugh said, the state supreme court would likely affirm Johnson's ruling.[60]

Some public bodies have also used the provision that discussion of legal matters may be discussed in secret to hide certain discussions from the public. The state's attorney general, however, has said that discussions of the law are not automatically exempt from public view. There must be "more than a desire to discuss general legal matters," the attorney general wrote. The statute "requires that there be a specific legal dispute or specific legal inquiry" before the discussion may be held in closed session.[61]

Any person, including a commonwealth's attorney acting in an official capacity, may initiate a legal action against a public body for violating the act. While a pattern of violations may be necessary for a court to take such a suit seriously,[62] the law provides

---

[59] *Id.* at 10.

[60] Telephone interview, October 29, 1991.

[61] 1986-87 Rep. A.G. 31. *See also* 1982-83 Rep. A.G. 716.

[62] *See, e.g.,* Marsh v. Richmond Newspapers, 288 S.E.2d 415, 422 (Va. 1982).

that a single violation of the act is sufficient to warrant penalties upon a board or public official.

A public official violating the act can be fined between $25 and $1,000. In addition, the court can require a public body to pay the legal expenses of the person bringing the action.

8. PROTECTING SOURCES AND INFORMATION

In its purest form, journalism is simply observation – the gathering of information from a variety of sources and the distribution of that information to people who want and need it. Sometimes the sources of the information need to keep their identities secret, and there is little debate over the proposition that, without the use of confidential sources, many important stories would go untold.[1] There *is* debate, however, over whether journalists have – or should have – a legal right to refuse to identify sources when asked to do so by law enforcement or other government agencies. And if they do have such a right, when should it yield to the needs of the government for the information?

The U.S. Supreme Court has recognized the importance of confidential sources to newsgathering, but has ruled that the First Amendment does not guarantee journalists the right to keep the identities of sources secret.[2] The Court has been clear in its proclamations that journalists have no rights not also

---

[1] The Virginia Supreme Court has noted, for example, that "as a news-gathering mechanism, a newsman's privilege of confidentiality of information and identity of his source is an important catalyst to the free flow of information guaranteed by the freedom of press clause of the First Amendment." Brown v. Commonwealth, 204 S.E.2d 429, 431 (Va. 1974).

[2] Branzburg v. Hayes, 408 U.S. 665, 690 (1972).

enjoyed by non-journalists.[3] Instead, the Court has left to the states the task of determining when – if at all – journalists are protected by a privilege allowing them to keep sources confidential.[4]

And a number of states have responded. Thirty-six states and the District of Columbia have passed laws – called "shield laws" – protecting journalists from being forced to reveal their sources unless state governments demonstrate a crucial need for the information.[5] The criteria many states use to balance a journalist's need to keep a source secret with the state's need for the identity of the source are tied to Justice Potter Stewart's dissenting opinion in *Branzburg v. Hayes,* the Supreme Court's landmark case involving confidential sources.[6] In that dissent,

---

[3] *Id.* at 667. *See also* Houchins v. KQED, 438 U.S. 1 (1978), and Pell v. Procunier, 417 U.S. 817 (1974), in which the Court refused to grant the press access to government property, in part because access could not also be granted to the public at large.

[4] *See, for example,* Winegard v. Oxberger, 258 N.W.2d 847 (Iowa 1977), *cert. denied,* 436 U.S. 905 (1978); State v. Sandstrom, 581 P.2d 812 (Kan. 1978), *cert. denied,* 440 U.S. 929 (1979); Maressa v. New Jersey Monthly, 445 A.2d 376 (N.J. 1982) *cert. denied,* 459 U.S. 907 (1982); and Brown v. Commonwealth, 204 S.E.2d 429 (Va. 1974), *cert. denied,* 419 U.S. 966 (1974), in which state supreme courts have upheld qualified privileges of keeping sources and information confidential, and the U.S. Supreme Court has let the state rulings stand by denying *certiorari.*

[5] *See* Anthony Fargo, *Confidential Sources and Information, in* COMUNICATION AND THE LAW 311 (W. Wat Hopkins ed., 2016 ed.)

[6] Justice Stewart was joined in his dissent by Justices William Brennan and Thurgood Marshall. 408 U.S. at 725 (Stewart, J., dissenting).

Justice Stewart suggested that reporters be required to reveal their confidential sources only if the government clearly demonstrates:[7]

- there is probable cause to believe the journalist has information clearly relevant to a specific, probable violation of law;
- the information sought cannot be obtained by alternative means less destructive of First Amendment rights;
- there is a compelling and overriding interest in the information.

Appellate courts have come to rely on the test by means of a serpentine route. In *Branzburg,* Justice Lewis Powell, who cast the deciding vote supporting the majority's position that the First Amendment does not grant to journalists the right to keep sources confidential, wrote a short concurring opinion noting that efforts by prosecutors to annex the media would not be tolerated. A proper balance should be struck between freedom of the press and the obligation on citizens to testify when called upon, Justice Powell wrote.[8]

Powell provided no guidelines for a test to balance these competing interests, however. He simply

---

[7] 408 U.S. at 743 (Stewart, J., dissenting). The majority is sometimes given credit for this three-part test, but the majority in *Branzburg* clearly did not endorse such a test. *See infra* notes 39-42 and accompanying text.

[8] *Id.* at 709-10 (Powell, J., concurring). An explication of Justice Powell's opinion with background can be found in Michele Bush Kimball, *The Intent Behind the Cryptic Concurrence That Provided a Reporter's Privilege,* 13 COMM. L & POL'Y 379 (2008).

wrote that journalists who believed subpoenas were not issued in good faith would have "access to the court on a motion to quash and an appropriate protective order may be entered." These controversies, Justice Powell suggested, would be determined on a case-by-case basis.[9] In the absence of a test from the Court or Justice Powell, then, lower appellate courts and legislatures have often turned to Stewart's dissent.

VIRGINIA STATE COURTS AND THE REPORTER'S PRIVILEGE

The Virginia General Assembly has passed no shield law, but the commonwealth still provides protection for confidential sources and information. In *Brown v. Commonwealth,*[10] the Virginia Supreme Court established a qualified privilege that – by intent or not – tracks Justice Stewart's guidelines.[11] In

---

[9] *Id.* at 710 (Powell, J., concurring). While Justice Powell provided no specific guidelines for a balancing test, courts have not hesitated to use his concurrence as a foundation for denying the privilege of confidentiality. *See, e.g.,* United States v. Model Magazine Distrib., Inc., 955 F.2d 229, 233 (4th Cir. 1992) (quoting Justice Powell's rejection of the Stewart test in denying a motion to quash a subpoena). *See also* Phillip Randolph Roach Jr., *The Newsman's Confidential Source Privilege in Virginia,* 22 U. RICH. L. REV. 377, 386-87 (1988), in which Justice Powell is given credit for a balancing test.

[10] 204 S.E.2d 429 (1974). Since *Brown,* a number states have recognized the privilege of confidentiality through case law. *See* Fargo, *supra* note 5, at 333.

[11] In his opinion for the court in *Brown,* Judge Richard Poff cited *Branzburg* but did not specifically cite Justice Stewart's dissenting opinion. Instead, he cited *Vermont v. St. Peter,* 315 A.2d 254 (Vt. 1974), in which the Vermont Supreme Court enunciated a test similar to the one Judge Poff established in *Brown.*

Brown, the court recognized that "as a news-gathering mechanism, a newsman's privilege of confidentiality of information and identity of his source is an important catalyst to the free flow of information guaranteed by the freedom of press clause of the First Amendment."[12]

The state court, however, agreed with the U.S. Supreme Court, holding that journalists have no First Amendment right to keep sources and information confidential. Such confidentiality is allowed only by the grant of a privilege by the commonwealth, the court held, and the privilege must yield to overriding governmental interests, such as effective law enforcement. "But," the court noted, "we think the privilege of confidentiality should yield only when the defendant's need is essential to a fair trial," a determination that must be made on a case-by-case basis.[13]

The need for confidential information is essential, the court held, and outweighs the journalist's privilege of confidentiality:[14]

- when the information is not available from alternative sources, and
- when one of three additional criteria is met:

+ the material is needed to prove any element of a criminal offense;

+ the material is needed to prove a defense asserted by the defendant; or

+ the material is needed to mitigate the penalty in the alleged crime.

---

[12] 204 S.E.2d at 431.

[13] *Id.*

[14] *Id.*

In *Brown,* the court held that the identity of the journalist's source was not essential to the case. The case began when the *Free Lance Star* of Fredericksburg published a story about a shooting death. Attorneys for the suspect in the murder wanted reporter Helaine Patterson to reveal the sources she used for the story, which reported details of the shooting that varied from official reports.[15]

The Virginia Supreme Court held that the identity of the source was irrelevant to the case since the inconsistencies were not material and, therefore, did not outweigh the journalist's privilege.[16]

FEDERAL COURTS IN VIRGINIA AND THE REPORTER'S PRIVILEGE

Federal courts have different rules than state courts, and the federal courts with jurisdiction over Virginia do not recognize a reporter's qualified privilege in criminal cases,[17] like *Brown.*

The most recent – and most explicit – holding on the matter came in 2013 and was related to the federal government's prosecution of Jeffrey A. Sterling, a former CIA employee who was charged with providing classified information to *New York Times* reporter James Risen. Risen was subpoenaed to provide the name of confidential sources upon whom he relied for his book *State of War: The Secret History of the CIA and the Bush Administration.*[18] The federal

---

[15] *Id.* at 430.

[16] *Id.* at 431.

[17] *See, e.g.,* United States v. Sterling, 724 F.3d 482, 492, 499 (4th Cir. 2013), *cert. denied* 134 S.Ct. 2696 (2014).

[18] *Id.* at 490-91.

court for the Eastern District of Virginia quashed the subpoena, holding that Risen had a qualified First Amendment privilege.[19] The Fourth U.S. Circuit Court of Appeals, however, overturned that holding:

> There is no First Amendment testimonial privilege, absolute or qualified, that protects a reporter from being compelled to testify by the prosecution or the defense in criminal proceedings about criminal conduct that the reporter personally witnessed or participated in, absent a showing of bad faith, harassment, or other such non-legitimate motive, even though the reporter promised confidentiality to the source.[20]

The court ruled that Risen had no privilege because he had personal knowledge of criminal activity, in this case, the leaking of classified government information. He was, therefore, in the same position as the journalists in *Branzburg*,[21] a case the Fourth Circuit interpreted as providing no privilege.[22]

The ruling did not upset the Fourth Circuit's 1986 decision in *Larouche v. National Broadcasting Co.*,[23] in which it held that reporters are protected from divulging identities of confidential sources in civil actions.

---

[19] United States v. Sterling, 818 F. Supp. 2d 945, 947 (E.D. Va. 2011).

[20] 724 F.3d at 492.

[21] *Id.*

[22] *Id.* at 495.

[23] 780 F.2d 1134 (4th Cir. 1986).

Lyndon Larouche sought the identity of a confidential source used by NBC to prepare two stories about him and his political organization.[24] In determining whether a journalist's privilege would protect sources in civil proceedings, the court held, a federal district court must apply a three-part test to balance the interests of the journalist against the needs of a party for the source identification. A court must determine whether: [25]

- the information is relevant,
- the information can be obtained by alternative means, and
- there is a compelling interest in the information.

Larouche, the court held, had not exhausted all his non-party depositions before seeking NBC's sources, and he knew the identities of all NBC's principal sources well before the two broadcasts.[26]

In addition, the federal court for the Eastern District of Virginia has indicated in two cases that news organizations may be protected from providing information even in the absence of a promise of confidentiality, though in both cases the courts involved required disclosure after applying the *Larouche* test.

In a case out of the Richmond Division of the Eastern District,[27] Judge Robert R. Merhige ruled that

---

[24] *Id.* at 1136-37.

[25] *Id.* at 1139.

[26] *Id.*

[27] *See* Chapter 2, notes 9-10 and accompanying text, and Table 2 for information about the various divisions of the U.S. District Court for the Eastern District of Virginia.

The Daily Press of Newport News could be compelled to provide unpublished photographs of an accident scene in a civil action brought against a rental company following an accident in which a construction worker was injured.[28] Judge Merhige found that a number of courts had recognized a qualified privilege allowing news organizations to refuse to provide non-confidential information because, "[T]he potential burden on the free flow of information caused by the disclosure of nonconfidential material is equivalent to the burden of revealing confidential information."[29] He ruled, however, that the photos were clearly relevant to the case, and there were no reasonable alternative means for obtaining the information. In addition, he found that compelled disclosure of the photos caused no significant burden on the newspaper.[30]

Oddly enough, the newspaper had voluntarily allowed the defendant in the lawsuit to examine the photographs to determine whether they might be of value. After examining the photographs, the defendant continued its effort to require the newspaper to provide the photographs for use in court. That continued effort, the court ruled, demonstrated that the photographs were important to the case.[31]

---

[28] Stickels v. Gen. Rental Co., Inc., 750 F. Supp. 729, 732 (E.D. Va. 1990).

[29] *Id. See also* Clemente v. Clemente, 56 Va. Cir. 530 (Cir. Ct. 2001) (Arlington County) (noting the importance of "protecting [] reporters from burdensome subpoenas which may stifle the free flow of information through the press").

[30] *Id.*

[31] *Id.*

The Norfolk Division of the Eastern District Court ruled similarly five years later. In *Frederico v. Lincoln Military Housing, LLC.*,[32] Magistrate Judge Douglas E. Miller applied the *Larouche* test and required WTKR TV in Hampton Roads to turn over non-confidential materials in its files, even though he recognized that sometimes such materials might be protected by a journalist's privilege.[33]

LAROUCHE, NON-CONFIDENTIAL SOURCES AND OTHER ISSUES IN VIRGINIA

The *Larouche* test has not been applied by a Virginia appellate court, though Richmond Circuit Judge T. J. Markow applied it in a controversial case involving Philip Morris and ABC. Judge Markow first required ABC to provide confidential information and reveal the identity of a source to the tobacco company, then reversed himself and upheld the network's claim of confidentiality. In his first ruling, Judge Markow applied the *Larouche* test and found that the (1) the information was clearly relevant to Philip Morris's claim that ABC broadcast with actual malice a story alleging that the tobacco company spiked cigarettes with nicotine, (2) that the information was available from no other source, and (3) there was a compelling

---

[32] 2014 WL 3962823, *1 (No. 2:12-CV-80) (E.D. Va. Aug. 13, 2014).

[33] *Id.* at *6. *See also* Gilbert v. Allied Chemical Corp., 411 F. Supp. 505, 511 (E.D. Va. 1976), *abrogated in part, Stickles,* 750 F. Supp. 729 (E.D. Va. 1990), in which the court required journalists to turn over files containing secondary materials gathered as part of their research,

interest in the information.[34] Judge Markow cited *Brown v Commonwealth,* but did not explain why he used the *Larouche* test rather than the *Brown* test. It could be that the *Phillip Morris* case was civil rather than criminal, or it could be that it was specifically a defamation case. The application of the test came immediately after Judge Markow had ruled that under the Constitution, "[T]he press enjoys a qualified privilege against disclosure of confidential sources in public figure defamation cases where the reporter is a defendant."[35] Therefore, he ruled, because "*Branzburg* allows for a reporter's qualified privilege against disclosure of confidential sources in public figure defamation actions, so too do the laws of the Commonwealth."[36] So, either the fact that the case was a civil case or because *Branzburg* pulled it within the gamut of the federal Constitution, Judge Markow applied *Larouche* rather than *Brown.*

Three days after he issued his ruling, Judge Markow ordered that it not be enforced and subsequently agreed to a rehearing on the matter.[37] More than six months later, Judge Markow held that Philip Morris needed to show that it had exhausted other "reasonably available sources" without locating

---

[34] Philip Morris Cos. v. American Broad. Cos., No. LX-816-3, 1995 WL 301428 ,*8-10 (opinion letter) (Richmond Cir., Jan. 26, 1995).

[35] *Id.* at *2.

[36] *Id.*

[37] *See Tobacco Companies Launch Barrage of Subpoenas Seeking Reporters' Records,* THE NEWS MEDIA & THE LAW, Winter 1995, at 4.

the information.[38] Markow allowed ABC to keep the information confidential, and the parties settled the case a month later.

In reversing himself, Judge Markow made what has become a common error. He wrote that, in *Branzburg v. Hayes,* "[T]he Supreme Court described a three part analysis that a court should make before declaring that confidential sources be disclosed."[39] The description of the three-part analysis came in Justice Stewart's dissenting opinion, not in the majority opinion.[40] The majority in *Branzburg* refused to grant to journalists a privilege not also enjoyed by other citizens[41] and, in doing so, had some harsh language for the claim that journalists deserved such a privilege.[42]

---

[38] Philip Morris Cos. v. American Broad. Cos., Inc., LX-816-3, 1995 WL 1055921, *3 (opinion letter) (Richmond Cir., July 11, 1995).

[39] *Id.*

[40] *See supra* note 7 and accompanying text. In addition, in the earlier opinion, Judge Markow attributed the Stewart test to Justice Powell, reporting, "The language in *Brown* [*v. Commonwealth*] echoes Justice Powell's concurrence in *Branzburg*." 1995 WL 301428, at *3.

[41] 408 U.S. 665, 690 (1972).

[42] *Id.* at 691-708. *See also,* Sterling v. Gen. Rental Co., Inc., 724 F.3d 482, 495-96 (4th Cir. 2013), in which the court emphsized that there is no support in *Branzburg* for the proposition that the case established – tacitly or purposefully – a qualified privilege for journalists to keep sources confidential.

Confidential Sources Tests

Stewart Test	*Brown Test*	*LaRouche Test*
There is probable cause to believe the journalist has information clearly relevant to a specific, probable violation of the law.		The information is clearly relevant.
The information sought cannot be obtained by alternative means less destructive of First Amendment rights.	The information being sought is not available from alternative sources.	The information cannot be obtained by alternative means.
There is a compelling and overriding interest in the information.	The material being sought is needed to prove any element of a criminal offense, or The material is needed to prove a defense asserted by the defendant, or The material is needed to mitigate the penalty in the alleged crime.	There is a compelling interest for the information.

The Virginia Supreme Court has not been asked to rule on attempts to gain access to unpublished notes, photographs and other materials that are not confidential. Such a ruling would be important since requests for unpublished materials are more frequent than requests for the identities of confidential sources.

At least two Virginia circuit courts have confronted the issue, however. In 2001, a judge for the Arlington Circuit implied that some non-confidential information may be withheld by news organizations, but, after applying the *Larouche* test, required that it be made available. "The fact that the information is not confidential tips the balance in favor of disclosure," Judge JoAnne F. Alper held.[43]

Ten years later, Norfolk Circuit Court Judge Everett A. Martin ruled that the *Virginian-Pilot* was required to allow a journalist to testify about matters that the reporter observed. The privilege provided in *Brown,* Judge Martin held, did not apply in the case because the material was not confidential.[44]

One other point needs to be made.

Journalists should be clear with both their sources and their editors or news directors about the nature and extent of promises of confidentiality. This has become increasingly important because of the U.S. Supreme Court's ruling in *Cohen v. Cowles Media, Inc.* in 1991.[45] In that case, the Court allowed damages to be assessed against a newspaper because the paper breached a promise of confidentiality. Reporters for the newspaper had promised confidentiality to a campaign worker in exchange for information about a candidate. Editors for the paper, however, decided that the more important story was that the campaign worker provided information to

---

[43] Clemente v. Clemente, 56 Va. Cir. 530 (Cir. Ct. 2001) (Arlington County).

[44] Commonwealth v. Jones, 82 Va. Cir. 379, 379 (Cir. Ct. 2011) (Norfolk City).

[45] 501 U.S. 663 (1991).

smear a candidate and ordered his name published over the objections of the reporters.[46]

Journalists should also avoid promising confidentiality to sources without discussing the ramifications of the promise with editors or news directors and learning the policy of their news organizations. Some news organizations, for example, require journalists to be willing to reveal the identities of sources to their supervisors before stories based on those sources will be published or broadcast.

Finally, journalists should be clear on what actions to take, questions to ask and responses to give when they receive requests for information and, more importantly, when they receive subpoenas demanding information or materials.

---

[46] *Id.* at 666.

9. Covering Courts in Virginia

The conflict between the Sixth Amendment right to a fair trial and the First Amendment right of a free press, the U.S. Supreme Court has noted, is "almost as old as the Republic."[1] These two rights are basic to a democratic society and are implicitly related: The Sixth Amendment provides that a person shall be treated fairly by the criminal justice system; the First Amendment ensures that the courts shall be open to public scrutiny so citizens can determine whether justice is being fulfilled. The conflict, as one Virginia scholar noted, "is not a clash between right and wrong, but between right and right. It is not a conflict between hero and villain, but between two heroes," making the issue very difficult to resolve.[2]

This issue has become compounded by the growth of high profile trials whose coverage dominates the news media. The media's role in the trial process is complex. Having a televised trial or even televised coverage of a trial creates a media narrative that emerges in addition to the actual case. In some respects this media trial becomes the actual trial, creating a public spectacle in which the real issue before the court is drowned out by media chatter. Media representation of trials elevates some issues

---

[1] Nebraska Press Ass'n. v. Stuart, 427 U.S. 539, 547 (1976).

[2] Sam G. Riley, The Free Press-Fair Trial Controversy: A Discussion of the Issues Involved and an Examination of Pre-Trial Publicity by Survey Research (1970) (unpublished doctoral dissertation, University of North Carolina at Chapel Hill). The late Dr. Riley is an emeritus professor of communication at Virginia Tech.

over others and makes even minor incidences part of larger contests for victory.

Traditionally, when First and Sixth Amendment rights have come into conflict, the parties involved have attempted to resolve their differences by taking one of two paths: adjudication in the courts or voluntary guidelines for covering trials and hearings.

Both paths have been taken in Virginia.

COURT-ESTABLISHED GUIDELINES

Trial judges in Virginia have considerable authority over conduct in their courtrooms. That authority includes the power to punish a person for critical remarks aimed at the judge, the power to exclude from the court any person the judge believes may be disruptive, and the power to change the location of a trial because of pre-trial publicity.

Contempt of Court

A judge's power to punish a person for contempt of court extends to punishment for any "vile, contemptuous or insulting language addressed to or published of a judge for or in respect of any act or proceeding."[3]

The Virginia Supreme Court has held that judges are not free from criticism, but when the critical remarks tend to destroy respect for the courts, the critic may be held in contempt.[4] The statute has rarely been invoked.

---

[3] VA. CODE ANN. §18.2-456 (1950).

[4] Weston v. Commonwealth, 77 S.E.2d 405, 409-10 (Va. 1953). *See, also,* In re McConnell, 370 U.S. 230 (1962); Offutt v. United States, 348 U.S. 11 (1954).

Closed Hearings & Trials

The media's right to cover court proceedings has a relatively short history in American law. The first major case involving the right to media access to courtrooms occurred in 1979 when a New York judge banned the press and public from a pretrial hearing in a 1976 case where a Rochester man was murdered on a fishing trip and thrown overboard into Seneca Lake.[5] A Rochester publisher of two newspapers, the *Democrat & Chronicle* and the *Times-Union,* brought suit for access claiming that under the First Amendment the press and public had a right to access the pre-trial proceedings, and that the public had a right to witness public trials as part of the fair trial language of the Sixth Amendment.[6] The U.S. Supreme Court in *Gannett Co. v. DePasquale* disagreed. Justice Potter Stewart, writing for the majority, held that it was within a judge's discretion to preserve a fair trial by denying the public, including the press, access to court proceedings. He found that the Sixth Amendment allowed the defendant the right to a public trial, but nowhere was there a constitutional right given to the public to attend trials.[7]

Virginia appellate courts are highly deferential to trial court judges' decision to manage media coverage in the courtroom. The Virginia Supreme Court examines a trial court judge's decision regarding media using the highly deferential "abuse of discretion

---

[5] Gannett Co. v. DePasquale, 443 U.S. 368 (1979).

[6] *Id.* at 391. It is important to note that the Sixth Amendment says nothing about media presence at trials, only that criminal defendants have a right to speedy and public trials.

[7] *Id.* at 387. Justice Stewart also noted that the Sixth Amendment's guarantee to a public trial only applied to criminal, not civil, trials.

standard."[8] Judges have been less hesitant in using a statute that allows them to close proceedings. Virginia law provides that:

> In the trial of all criminal cases, whether the same be felony or misdemeanor cases, the court may, in its discretion, exclude from the trial any persons whose presence would impair the conduct of a fair trial, provided that the right of the accused to a public trial shall not be violated.[9]

Using this statute as a basis, judges have not hesitated to exclude the press from courtrooms, sometimes indiscriminately. They have done so, even though the U.S. Supreme Court, using a Virginia case as its vehicle, has established that trials may be closed only in rare circumstances. In *Richmond Newspapers, Inc. v. Virginia,* the Court held that the First Amendment requires trials to be open unless there is some overriding government interest that mandates closure.[10] And, the Court found that, such an interest must be clearly articulated in writing by the trial judge.[11] In *Richmond Newspapers*, a criminal defendant was tried three times for the stabbing death of a hotel clerk; the first trial's conviction was reversed, the second and third trials ended in mistrial. At the outset of the fourth trial the judge, excluded the media from the courtroom, citing the fact that the high level of publicity surrounding the trial could influence

---

[8] Virginia Broad. Corp. v. Commonwealth, 749 S.E.2d 313, 318 (Va. 2013).

[9] VA. CODE ANN. § 19.2-266 (1950).

[10] 448 U.S. 555, 564-65 (1980).

[11] *Id.* at 581.

jurors. Richmond Newspapers sued and ultimately the issue of press coverage of trials reached the U.S. Supreme Court in 1980.[12] Exactly one year after *Gannett*, Chief Justice Warren Burger wrote that there is a First Amendment right for the press and public to trials justified by a long history of Anglo-American tradition and jurisprudence.[13] However, the Court recognized this access was not absolute and that a judge could make restrictions on the presence of the public and press "in the fair administration of justice."[14] Any action, however, must be made of the least restrictive means, which mandates that the judge cannot exclude the media unless there are no other less restrictive measures to safeguard the rights of the defendant. Chief Justice Burger's decision states that this media access to trials actually helps defendants in that open trials facilitate truth and factfinding in cases.[15]

In 1981, the Virginia Supreme Court, following the precepts of *Richmond Newspapers*, established a series of guidelines to help trial courts resolve conflicts involving access to criminal proceedings. The case, *Richmond Newspapers, Inc. v. Commonwealth*[16] is often called *Richmond Newspapers II* to distinguish it from the earlier case involving the same newspaper company.[17]

---

[12] *Id.*

[13] *Id.* at 565-70.

[14] *Id.* at 581 n.18.

[15] *Id.* at 596.

[16] 281 S.E.2d 915 (Va. 1981).

[17] At the state level, *Richmond Newspapers, Inc. v. Virginia* was also identified as *Richmond Newspapers, Inc. v. Commonwealth*. "*Richmond Newspapers I*" and "*Richmond Newspapers II,*" therefore, are used to distinguish the two cases.

Richmond Newspapers II consolidated three murder cases in which trial judges had summarily closed pretrial proceedings to the public and press.[18] The Virginia Supreme Court ruled that hearings in Virginia are presumed to be open and that none of the hearings should have been closed.[19] Unlike *Richmond Newspapers I,* the second case never reached the U.S. Supreme Court.[20]

The Virginia Supreme Court began its opinion in *Richmond Newspapers II* by noting that Virginians are guaranteed fair trials by both the Sixth Amendment of the federal Constitution and Article I, Section 8 of the Virginia Constitution.[21] But, the court noted, "A necessary adjunct to a fair trial is an open trial. The presence of the public will ensure that an accused's rights are not denied."[22] Openness, the court held, may improve the quality of testimony, encourage unknown witnesses to come forward with relevant

---

[18] 281 S.E.2d at 917 n.1.

[19] *Id.* at 925.

[20] *Richmond Newspapers II* involved pretrial hearings, but the guidelines established by the court are based on *Richmond Newspapers I*, and much of the language of the opinion relates to trials. The guidelines, therefore apparently apply to the closing of trials as well as pretrial hearings. Indeed, the Virginia Court of Appeals applied the guidelines to the closure of trials in the case of *In re Times-World Corp.*, 373 S.E.2d 474 (Va. Ct. App. 1988).

[21] Both the Sixth Amendment to the U.S. Constitution and the Virginia Constitution provide that a defendant have a speedy and public trial, be informed of the nature of the charges, be allowed to confront witnesses and be allowed to produce evidence.

[22] 281 S.E.2d at 920.

information and cause participants to perform their duties more conscientiously.[23]

While adverse publicity can affect the fairness of trial proceedings, access to pretrial hearings is as important as access to trials, the court noted.[24] Such hearings are often the only adversary proceedings for an accused, and the public has the right to determine for itself whether the proper balance is struck between preventing misconduct on the part of the judicial system and the possibility that a guilty person may go free. "To allow the public to view the trial without any knowledge of what has taken place previously," the court held, "would make the right of access a hollow one."[25]

Therefore, the court ruled, absent "an overriding interest articulated in the findings," pretrial hearings, like trials, shall be open to the public, a rule mandated by the Virginia Constitution.[26]

The language used by the state high court came from the U.S. Supreme Court's opinion in *Richmond Newspapers.* The state court noted, however, that the earlier case did not establish a test for determining what might be a "overriding interest." The court, therefore, adopted the rule that hearings would be open unless the information released in those hearings, which would not otherwise reach jurors, would jeopardize the defendant's right to a fair trial. In addition, the state court held a trial judge should consider alternative measures before closing a hearing and, if closure is required, should only close that

---

[23] *Id.* at 921.
[24] *Id.* at 922.
[25] *Id.*
[26] *Id.*

portion of the hearing in which the prejudicial information would be introduced.[27]

The court also held that, before a hearing is closed, members of the public should have the opportunity to object. The court, therefore, established procedures trial courts should follow:[28]

- Motions to close hearings should be made in writing and filed with the court before the day of the hearing; the public must be given reasonable notice that a closure hearing will be conducted.
- The burden is on the party seeking closure to show that an open hearing would jeopardize the defendant's right to a fair trial.
- The party objecting to closure has the burden of showing that reasonable alternatives to closure are available.
- The judge must write an opinion explaining his findings and, if allowing closure, explaining why the alternative measures would not work.
- The judge may receive information outside the hearing of the public and the jury to determine whether its release would be prejudicial

The Virginia Court of Appeals follows a two-part test developed by the U.S. Supreme Court in *Press-Enterprise Co. v. Superior Court*[29] to determine when the public has a First Amendment right of access to a hearing or trial. In *Press-Enterprise Co.* the Court held that trial courts must ask two questions to determine when court proceedings should be open: (1) "whether the place and process have historically been open to

---

[27] *Id.* at 923.
[28] *Id.* at 924.
[29] 478 U.S. 1, 8 (1986).

the press and general public," and (2) "whether public access plays a significant positive role in the functioning of the particular process in question."[30] If the court finds that the proceedings have been historically open and that the public plays a role then there is a strong presumption that the proceedings should be open. Using the test, the Virginia Court of Appeals ruled that one trial judge erroneously closed jury *voir dire* in a criminal case,[31] and that another trial judge erroneously closed a competency hearing for a murder suspect.[32] However, the court also held that because the purpose of a discovery hearing has traditionally been to prepare for trial, documents subpoenaed and used in such a hearing were not judicial records subject to a right of access.[33]

The *Press-Enterprise* case began when the newspaper company was denied access to a pre-trial hearing in a death penalty murder case. The California Magistrate Court had refused the press both access to the 41-day preliminary hearing and to the transcript. Again writing for the majority, Chief Justice Burger held that there was a First Amendment right of access to preliminary hearings by the press and that California had a long history of such access.[34] Moreover, Chief Justice Burger held that public access is even more important when a proceeding is without a jury and is conducted by a judge only. The court held that the

---

[30] *Id.* at 8.

[31] In re Times-World Corp., 373 S.E.2d 474 (Va. App. 1988).

[32] In re Times-World Corp., 488 S.E.2d 677 (Va. App. 1997).

[33] In re Worrell Enterprises, Inc., 419 S.E.2d 271 (Va. App. 1992).

[34] 478 U.S. at 10.

only way a judge could deny access to a preliminary hearing was make findings on the record of how access would harm the justice process and how this restriction was narrowly tailored to preserve this goal.[35]

Not all the Virginia Supreme Court's rulings have favored openness. In a disturbing opinion handed down in April 2000, the court, by a 4-3 vote, affirmed the closure of preliminary hearings in a murder trial and a sexual assault trial because attorneys for the media used a legal remedy the court found to be inappropriate.[36] Attorneys used a writ of mandamus in an effort to compel the judges in the cases to keep open the preliminary hearings. They did so after the judges refused to delay closure in order to hear objections from attorneys for the media. The state supreme court held that mandamus "is an extraordinary remedy" that should be used only in urgent circumstances, and it was inappropriate.[37] Justice Lawrence L. Koontz, joined by Justices Elizabeth B. Lacy and Cynthia D. Kinser, dissented. Justice Koontz wrote that the trial court did not give sufficient consideration to the First Amendment access rights of the media and that "the right of access of the news media to court proceedings is a hollow one without an effective remedy when that right is wrongfully decided."[38] Koontz would have granted the writ.

In addition, the Virginia Supreme Court has held that there is a presumption that civil trials and records will be open, unless there is "an interest so compelling

---

[35] *Id.* at 13-15.

[36] Hertz v. Times-World Corp., 528 S.E.2d 458 (Va. 2000).

[37] *Id.* at 462.

[38] *Id.* at 466 (Koontz, J., dissenting).

that it cannot be protected reasonably by some measure" other than closure.[39]

Pre-Trial Publicity & Change of Venue

One method of helping ensure that a defendant receives a fair trial in the face of overwhelming publicity, the U.S. Supreme Court has noted, is to change the venue, that is, to move the trial to a location where the publicity has not been as great.[40]

Changes of venue, however, cause many problems. Attorneys, witnesses and other trial participants must physically relocate for the duration of the trial, causing added expense and inconvenience. In addition, the U.S. Constitution provides that a person be tried in the "district wherein the crime shall have been committed."[41] Judges, therefore, do not like to change the venue unless absolutely necessary.

That has been particularly true in Virginia. The Virginia Supreme Court has held that the law presumes that a defendant will get a fair trial from the citizens of the city or county where the crime was committed. This presumption, the court held, must be overcome by a clear showing of widespread prejudice against the defendant.[42]

---

[39] Shenandoah Publ'g House, Inc. v. Fanning, 368 S.E.2d 253, 256 (Va. 1988).

[40] *See, e.g.,* Sheppard v. Maxwell, 384 U.S. 333 (1966); Rideau v. Louisiana, 373 U.S. 723 (1963).

[41] U.S. CONSTITUTION amend. 6.

[42] Coppola v. Commonwealth, 257 S.E.2d 797, 801 (Va. 1972), *cert. denied*, 444 U.S. 1103 (1980). *See also*, Asher v. Commonwealth, 408 S.E.2d 906, 911 (Va. Ct. App. 1991), *cert. denied*, 506 U.S. 865 (1992); Gray v. Commonwealth, 356 S.E.2d 157, 168 (Va. 1987), *cert. denied* 484 U.S. 873 (1987); Pope v. Commonwealth, 360 S.E.2d 352, 356 (Va. 1987), *cert. denied*,

It is insufficient, the court held, that jurors know about the crime because of publicity. Indeed, even a large amount of publicity about a case or defendant, standing alone, is insufficient cause for a change of venue.[43] This seems to be particularly true when the reporting on the case is neither inaccurate nor intemperate.[44]

VOLUNTARY GUIDELINES

A number of states have adopted guidelines suggesting the types of information about crimes or criminal suspects that should or should not be released.[45] There have been rare cases in which courts have required journalists to adhere to these voluntary bench-bar-press guidelines.[46] The U.S. Supreme Court has made it clear, however, that such gag orders on the press are unconstitutional,[47] even though trial judges may place gag orders on participants in a trial. Judges sometimes use bench-bar-press guidelines in structuring those gag orders.

Virginia's "Guidelines on Release of Information to the News Media," like those of most states, are

---

485 U.S. 1015 (1988); Stockton v. Commonwealth, 314 S.E.2d 371, 380 (Va. 1984), *cert. denied*, 469 U.S. 873 (1984).

[43] Briley v. Commonwealth, 273 S.E.2d 48, 52 (Va. 1980), *cert. denied*, 451 U.S. 1031 (1981).

[44] *Id. See also, Stockton*, 314 S.E.2d at 380.

[45] Good discussions of voluntary guidelines appear *in* Glenelle Belmas & Wayne Overbeck, MAJOR PRINCIPLES OF MEDIA LAW (1st ed. 2015); Kent R. Middleton & William E. Lee, THE LAW OF PUBLIC COMMUNICATION (9th ed., 2013); Derigan Silver, *Access to Courts, in* COMMUNICATION AND THE LAW 329-62 (W. Wat Hopkins ed. 2016).

[46] *See, e.g.*, Federated Publ'ns v. Swedberg, 633 P.2d 74 (Wash. 1981), *cert. denied*, 456 U.S. 984 (1982).

[47] *See, e.g.,* Nebraska Press Ass'n v. Stuart, 427 U.S. 539, 570 (1976).

based on the American Bar Association Standards on Fair Trial and Free Press, adopted by the ABA House of Delegates in 1966 and revised in 1980.[48] The guidelines apply to all employees of the Virginia Judicial System and to all circuit court clerks and their employees.

The Virginia guidelines identify as "releasable" the following information:

- Factual background information about an accused, including name, age, address, employment and family status.
- The substance or text of the charge.
- The fact that the accused denies the charge, if appropriate.
- Any action taken by a judge in open court.
- Anything in official records which have not been sealed by a judge.

The following types of information are identified as "unreleasable":

- Statements about the character or reputation of the accused.
- The contents of any statements by the accused, except a denial of the charges, including possible alibis, admissions or confessions, or the refusal of the accused to make a statement.

---

[48] *See, e.g.,* Guidelines on Release of Information to the News Media, http://worldcat.org/arcviewer/1/LEGAL/2007/06/27/0000067900/viewer/file1.html (accessed Jan. 6, 2016); Michael Downey, *Ethical Rules for Litigating in the Court of Public Opinion*, American Bar Association, Jul. 18, 2012, *available at* http://apps.americanbar.org/litigation/committees/ethics/email/summer2012/summer2012-0712-ethical-rules-litigating-court-public-opinion.html.

- The results of any tests or the refusal of the accused to participate in any tests.
- Statements about the character, reputation or credibility of any prospective witnesses or statements about the anticipated testimony of any witnesses.
- The possibility of a guilty plea or plea bargain.
- Opinions concerning the evidence or arguments in the case, including statements about what evidence may or may not be used.
- Prior criminal records, except as part of the release of public documents.

ELECTRONIC COVERAGE OF TRIALS AND HEARINGS

Ironically, the same section of the Code of Virginia which has allowed judges to exclude the press and public from courtrooms also allows journalists to photograph or electronically record those proceedings. As of July 1, 1992, cameras and tape recorders have been allowed in courtrooms in the commonwealth, with certain restrictions.

The first effort to win approval for cameras in Virginia courtrooms came in the 1970s, but it wasn't until 1987 that the General Assembly amended a ban on photographic equipment in the courtrooms to provide for a two-year experiment. [49] The experiment allowed electronic coverage of the Virginia Supreme Court, the Virginia Court of Appeals, two circuit

---

[49] A good history of Virginia's experience with cameras in courtrooms is in Teresa Keller, Cameras in Courtrooms: An Analysis of Television Court Coverage in Virginia (1992) (unpublished Ph.D. dissertation, University of Tennessee, Knoxville). Dr. Keller is a professor of mass communication at Emory and Henry College.

courts and two district courts. The experiment was expanded to include an additional circuit court.[50]

Then, in February 1992, despite two scathing denunciations of the experiment by the Virginia Supreme Court,[51] the general assembly adopted a bill allowing photographic coverage of all courts in the commonwealth.[52]

The coverage is neither absolute nor automatic.

A trial judge, for example, has the power under the law to prohibit or interrupt photographic coverage of a trial or to restrict coverage "as he deems appropriate to meet the ends of justice."[53] The law also specifies that the judge must inform the parties in a case of the possibility that the trial will be photographed by media representatives and allow them to object. An objection by a party does not require a judge to prohibit electronic coverage of a trial or hearing. Such an objection would be considered, among other factors, by the presiding judge.

The law prohibits photographic coverage of proceedings involving adoptions, juveniles, child custody, divorces, spousal support, sexual offenses, motions to suppress evidence and trade secrets. In addition, jurors, police informants, minors, undercover agents, victims of sexual offenses and families of victims of sexual offenses may not be photographed.

---

[50] In 1987, photography was allowed in the circuit courts in Bedford County and Virginia Beach and the district courts in Caroline County and Charlottesville. Later, the circuit court in Henrico County was added to the experiment.

[51] The reports were issued to Gov. Charles Robb in 1987 and Gov. Douglas Wilder in 1992.

[52] Senate Bill 480 amended VA. CODE ANN. § 19.2-266 (1950).

[53] VA. CODE ANN. § 19.2-266 (1950).

At no time can a recording be made of any conversation between attorneys and their clients, between co-counsel, between adverse parties, or between lawyers and the presiding judge. Finally, there may be no photographic or sound coverage of any conferences involving attorneys or the judge, or any conferences held at the judge's bench or in the judge's chambers.

The law also places restrictions on electronic equipment and media personnel necessary to operate that equipment. It specifies that equipment not be intrusive or distracting. No artificial lights are allowed, and neither cameras nor audio equipment may make distracting sounds. Microphones and wiring for audio equipment must be located in positions approved in advance by the presiding judge. Audio equipment is only allowed if the existing audio system is not suitable for broadcasting.

In addition, the law provides that no more than two television cameras with appropriate personnel; one still photographer with no more than two cameras, each having no more than two lenses, and no more than one audio system are permitted in any courtroom at any one time. As a result, media personnel must pool resources. And, the law states, the media must work out any pooling arrangements "without calling upon the presiding judge to mediate any dispute."

Media representatives are not prohibited from talking with presiding judges. Indeed, the law provides that the Virginia Association of Broadcasters and the Virginia Press Association designate one television journalist, one radio broadcaster and one still photographer to act as representatives of the media in making pooling arrangements and speaking with presiding judges about the coverage of any proceedings, including the location of equipment within courtrooms.

The law prohibits camera personnel from entering or leaving courtrooms, except during recesses, once proceedings begin and prohibits the movement of equipment in or out, without the judge's permission, except prior to or at the end of the proceedings or during the luncheon recess.

In June 1992, the Virginia Association of Broadcasters and the Virginia Press Association responded to the law with a memorandum circulated to their members listing "Courtroom Electronic Journalism Procedures Effective July 1, 1992." The procedures note that "a high degree of cooperation and coordination" will be required between "news agencies that are far more familiar with competition." These guidelines were updated by the Virginia Press Association and the Virginia Association of Broadcasters in 2013.[54] Specifically, the procedures require that:

- Media organizations require any person assigned to cover a trial proceeding to read the statute and to be briefed on the courtroom procedures.
- Organizations ask the proceeding judge in a specific case to allow electronic coverage of the proceedings in the case.
- Multiple requests to cover a particular case be referred to an area coordinator so pooling arrangements can be developed. The Associated Press and United Press International will be asked to run advisories over the state wire so other media can participate.

---

[54] 2013 Guidelines: Cameras in the Courtroom, http://www.vpa.net/cameras-courtroom (accessed Jan. 7, 2016).

The guidelines establish dress codes for still photographers, broadcast operators, and reporters covering trials. And they identify official media representatives across the state.[55]

SOCIAL MEDIA USE DURING TRIALS

The role of media in trials has changed in the past decade with the proliferation of social media, smart phones and tablets. Of course, a reporter's access to these technologies depends largely upon the rules concerning technology in the courtroom. Bans on cell phones in court are common in Virginia. Courts in Norfolk, Fairfax County, Montgomery County, Virginia Beach and other jurisdictions, for example, have an outright ban on cell phones in court for all attendees. This ban is controversial. Citing security concerns sheriff's deputies turn away people who come to court with cell phones despite the fact that the phones may contain important information.[56] However, the concern over cell phones and court disruptions are not unfounded. In 2013, a Virginia Beach lawyer was sued for defamation when he posted on Facebook a photo taken of another attorney and a criminal defendant. The photo was posted with a caption that read, "Notice the stain on this guys jail suit when he realized who he had as an attorney." The lawyer in the photo sued for defamation alleging his

---

[55] *Id.*

[56] *See* Patrick Wilson, *Safety Vies With Practicality in Courthouse Phone Ban*, VIRGINIAN-PILOT, Aug. 9, 2013, *available at* http://www.pilotonline.com/news/government/local/safety-vies-with-practicality-in-courthouse-phone-ban/article_dd37bfb4-b6f5-5419-838b-701fdd55b9a5.html.

professional reputation was damaged by the comment.[57]

Social media and smart technology are not just issues for courtroom antics. Many people use social media as a means of research. In many instances, jurors have used social media and hand-held devices to conduct research on trials, investigate plaintiffs and defendants, and express their personal opinions about specific court cases.[58] This type of behavior can lead to mistrials because unauthorized communication between jurors and the public constitutes a violation of parties' Sixth Amendment rights. A juror in a federal trial court in Pennsylvania used Twitter and Facebook to post that the jury had reached a verdict. The posts were picked up by a local radio station and broadcast during morning drive time.[59] However, the use of social media by jurors is not automatically grounds for a mistrial in some jurisdictions. In Alabama, a juror's social media relationships with the district attorney's office was not grounds for a mistrial in a rape case, nor was the failure to disclose these relationships during voir dire grounds for a new trial. Citing the Kentucky Supreme Court's holding that social media

---

[57] *See* Kathy Hiett, *Lawyer's Facebook Photo no Laughing Matter in Beach*, VIRGINIAN-PILOT, July 5, 2013, *available at* http://www.pilotonline.com/news/local/crime/lawyer-s-facebook-post-no-laughing-matter-in-beach/article_c3e91336-dec3-5e18-8db3-ad562b701ac2.html. It is important to note that lawyers and other court personnel are allowed to have cell phones and other portable electronics in the courtroom with them.

[58] *See, e g.*, United States v. Fumo, 639 F. Supp. 2d 544 (E.D. Pa., 2009); Wingus v. F/V Sirius Inc., 665 F. Supp. 2d 23 (D.Me. 2009); Juror No. One v. Cal., 206 Cal.App. 4th 854 (2012); State v. Tennessee, 418 S.W.3d 38 (Tenn. 2013).

[59] United States v. Fumo, 639 F. Supp. 2d 544 (E.D. Pa., 2009).

relationships were no the same as personal relationships, the Alabama Supreme Court held that social media friending or following did not constitute a conflict of interest that a that would preclude a juror from serving.[60]

Although no Virginia court has directly ruled on juror social media use, it stands to reason that Virginia courts would follow the national trend that evaluates juror social media use on a case-by-case basis. However, the use of social media by jurors in a case begs the question of social media use by reporters during trials.

Suppose a journalist used a smartphone to live tweet updates about a trial while witnessing the trial? That is exactly what the trial judge allowed during the high profile trial of former Penn State football coach Jerry Sandusky. In that case, the judge expressly permitted members of the media to bring electronic devices into the courtroom during the trial to live tweet or blog.[61] Similarly, the federal judge allowed reporters to live tweet during the trial of famed Irish Mafia boss James "Whitey" Bulger.[62] What these cases have in common is that the reporters were allowed to use social media because the judge issued a pre-trial order allowing them to do so. Reporters

---

[60] W.G.M. v. Alabama, 140 So.3d 491 (Ala. 2013)(citing Sluss v. Commonwealth of Ky., 381 S.W.3d 215 (Ky. 2012)).

[61] *See, e.g.*, Steve Myers, *Judge Allows Live-Tweeting, Live-Blogging During Jerry Sandusky Trial*, POYNTER, May 30, 2012, http://www.poynter.org/news/mediawire/175596/judge-allows-live-tweeting-live-blogging-during-jerry-sandusky-trial/.

[62] *See, e.g.,* Paige Williams, *Whitey Bulger: The Twitter Trial Narrative, by the Boston Globe's Kevin Cullen,* NEIMANSTORYBOARD, June 17, 2013, http://niemanstoryboard.org/stories/whitey-bulger-the-twitter-trial-narrative-by-the-boston-globes-kevin-cullen/.

covering cases should first ask permission to use social media during the trial process. As with all forms of media it is ultimately up to the judge to make the decision of whether social media can be used in a courtroom.[63]

---

[63] For more information regarding social media use in courtrooms *see, e.g.*, Emily Janoski-Haehlen, *The Courts are All a "Twitter": The Implications of Social Media Use in the Courts,* 46 VAL. U. L. REV. 43 (2011); Michael Lackey & Joseph Minta, *Lawyers and Social Media: The Legal Ethics of Tweeting, Facebooking and Blogging*, 28 TOURO L. REV. 149 (2012).

10. ADVERTISING REGULATION

Advertising – commercial speech – is protected by both the First Amendment to the U.S. Constitution and the Virginia Constitution – but that protection is limited.

Commercial speech, the U.S. Supreme Court has said, is different from other forms of protected speech, because advertisers can easily evaluate "the accuracy of their messages and the lawfulness of the underlying activity," and because "commercial speech, the offspring of economic self-interest, is a hardy breed of expression that is not 'particularly susceptible to being crushed by overbroad regulation.'"[1] Because of these differences, and to protect consumers from deception, the Supreme Court has allowed greater regulation of commercial speech.[2]

Virginia has taken advantage of the Court's flexibility in this area of mass communication law and has implemented a wide variety of regulations on advertising.

TRUTH IN ADVERTISING

Virginia law regulating commercial speech is wide-ranging. The commonwealth prohibits the use of false, deceptive or misleading advertisements in general – the prohibition is against any false or deceptive advertising about "anything offered" by a company, organization or individual.[3] The criminal statute is part of Virginia's anti-fraud provisions,

---

[1] Central Hudson Gas & Electric Corp. v. Pub. Serv. Comm'n. of New York, 447 U.S. 557, 564 n.6 (1980).

[2] *Id.* at 578.

[3] VA. CODE ANN. § 18.2-216 (1950).

however, and has been held only to apply to written advertisements.[4]

State law doesn't stop with this broad prohibition, however. It also prohibits deceptive advertising in a variety of specific areas, including food and restaurants, dentistry, the health professions, insurance policies and insurance company trade practices, automobiles and the source of any sales merchandise.[5]

Similarly, the advertising of certain merchandise – obscene materials, drug paraphernalia, illegal alcohol and electronic eavesdropping equipment,[6] for example – is prohibited, and the advertising of other products is regulated.

In addition, state law strictly regulates the use of some common advertising terms and descriptors. For example, the terms "secondhand," "irregular,"[7] "wholesale,"[8] "going out of business,"[9] "sterling,"[10] "coin silver,"[11] "market value," "suggested retail price," "manufacturer's suggested price," "list price"

---

[4] *See* Henry v. R.K. Chevrolet, Inc., 254 S.E.2d 66 (Va. 1979).

[5] VA. CODE ANN. §§ 3.2-5120-3.2-5127 (1950) (food and restaurants); VA. CODE ANN. §54.1-2706 (1950) (dentistry); VA. CODE ANN.§ 54.1-2403 (1950) (health professions); VA. CODE ANN. §§ 38.2-502 & 38.2-503 (1950) (insurance); VA. CODE ANN. § 46.2-1581 (1950) (automobiles);VA. CODE ANN. § 18.2-222 (1950) (sales merchandise).

[6] VA. CODE ANN. § 18.2-376 (1950) (obscene materials); VA. CODE ANN. §18.2-255.1 (1950) (drug paraphernalia); VA. CODE ANN. § 4.1-320 (1950) (illegal alcohol); VA. CODE ANN. § 19.2-63 (1950) (eavesdropping equipment).

[7] VA. CODE ANN. § 18.2-218 (1950).

[8] VA. CODE ANN. § 18.2-220 (1950).

[9] VA. CODE ANN. § 18.2-223 (1950).

[10] VA. CODE ANN. § 18.2-233 (1950).

[11] VA. CODE ANN. § 18.2-234 (1950).

and similar terms[12] must be used accurately, under penalty of law. And only genuine Smithfield hams – hams cured by the long-cure, dry salt method, aged for six months and processed within the city limits of Smithfield – may be advertised as "Smithfield hams."[13] Virginia laws against false advertising should be taken seriously. Along with civil lawsuits, violations of these laws can result in criminal charges.[14]

Advertising Techniques and Methods

Virginia also regulates a variety of advertising techniques and methods, ranging from bait-and-switch tactics to comparison advertising. Most of the regulations apply to businesses and organizations, rather than to individuals, and few of them apply directly to the mass media. They are important, however, because they affect the types of messages that may or may not be communicated to potential consumers. The law also prohibits the use of a person's name or likeness in an advertisement without permission or, if the person is dead, without permission of survivors.[15] Finally, the commonwealth also regulates political advertising.

It is important to note that the regulation of false advertising is unique. Unlike fraud, which requires a plaintiff to show a representation was patently untrue, false advertising occurs when an ad "contains a representation that, although deceptive or

---

[12] Va. Code Ann. § 59.1-207.4 (1950).

[13] Va. Code Ann. §§ 3.2-5419-3.2-5421 (1950).

[14] Va. Code Ann. § 3.2-5126 (1950).

[15] Va. Code Ann. § 18.2-216.1 (1950). This statute is discussed in greater detail in Chapter 6.

misleading, is not necessarily false or untrue."[16] Moreover, false advertising is not predicated on the truth of a "preexisting fact;" rather, false advertising claims are based on a false "promise" that cannot be fulfilled.[17]

Commercial Advertising

Virginia law requires businesses to be able to substantiate any price comparisons they make – whether those comparisons are to goods and services previously provided by the businesses or to goods and services offered by competitors. Specifically, businesses offering goods or services at sales prices must also be able to show that a substantial number of sales were made at the higher prices.[18] And businesses making comparisons to competitors must be able to show that the comparison is in fact to the competitor's prices for "substantially the same kind and quality" of goods and services.[19]

Auto dealers come under what may be the strictest regulatory scheme in state law. Two pages of the Virginia Code regulate language used to advertise both new and used cars. Regulations cover the use of a variety of terms, including "new," "sticker price," "at cost," "manufacturer's factory invoice" and "free."[20]

Most of the regulations apply strictly to automobile dealers, but individuals are required to

---

[16] Parker-Smith v. STO Corp., 551 S.E.2d 615, 619 (Va. 2001).

[17] *Id.*

[18] VA. CODE ANN. § 59.1-207.41 (1950).

[19] VA. CODE ANN. § 59.1-207.42 (1950).

[20] VA. CODE ANN. § 46.2-1581 (1950).

accurately report the make, year, model and options available on cars they are selling.[21]

Virginia law also requires that pay-per-service telephone operations – 900 numbers that are commonly advertised by television stations – must meet specific guidelines. Advertising of pay-per-service operations must include the per-minute cost of each call, along with the average length a call takes in order to benefit from the service. In addition, at the beginning of each call, the caller must be told the rate being charged.[22]

Finally, the law prohibits bait-and-switch tactics. The failure of a business to provide goods or services at advertised prices, the law says, is evidence of false or misleading advertising.[23]

As previously indicated, most advertising regulation applies to advertisers – that is, to the businesses, organizations or individuals selling goods and services – rather than to the mass media. Indeed, the law provides protection for radio and television stations, newspapers and other media organizations that unintentionally publish false or misleading advertising. A publisher of false advertising cannot be found guilty under state law if the publication was based upon copy of information provided by an advertiser or by the provider of goods and services.[24]

Media organizations, therefore, are under no obligation to verify all the information in potential advertisements – whether display or classified – before publishing those advertisements. Only when the copy

---

[21] VA. CODE ANN. § 18.2-221 (1950).
[22] VA. CODE ANN. § 59.1-430 (1950).
[23] VA. CODE ANN. § 18.2-217 (1950).
[24] VA. CODE ANN. § 3.2-5126 (1950).

of an advertisement is obviously suspect, does a media organization become liable for its publication.

In addition, the law provides that honest mistakes cannot be the basis of a false advertising claim,[25] so advertisers themselves are not liable when advertisements are false, if the advertisements were written and published in good faith. There are exceptions to this rule, however.[26] Plaintiffs must bring a false advertising claim within two years.[27]

Political Advertising

Political advertising regulation has a long history in the United States.[28] Recently, campaign finance laws have increased the amount of money a corporation can spend during a campaign. Virginia laws concerning campaign advertisements, however, are not as numerous as federal laws,[29] in part because campaign advertising is largely regulated by the Federal Elections Commission. Virginia campaign advertising laws are more tailored to limit locations of advertising and criminalize advertisements that may lead to voter disenfranchisement.

Virginia law has a false advertising component to campaign information. It is a criminal offense to disseminate information that is knowingly false in

---

[25] VA. CODE ANN. § 18.2-243 (1950).

[26] *See* discussion accompanying *infra* notes 46-50.

[27] VA. CODE ANN. § 8.01-248 (1950).

[28] For a detailed history of U.S. political advertising history, *see* Cayce Myers & Ruthann Lariscy, *Commercial Speech, Protected Speech, and Political Public Relations*, 39 PUB. REL. REV. 332 (2013).

[29] *See, e.g.,* McCutcheon v. FEC, 134 S.Ct. 1434 (2014); Citizens United v. FEC, 558 U.S. 310 (2010).

order to hinder a voter's ability to vote.[30] Likewise, solicitation of votes through offering voters money incentives is illegal.[31] There are even restrictions on where political advertising can take place. Campaigning at locations where citizens register to vote is strictly prohibited. However, campaign literature may be handed out if the campaign workers do so outside of the registration building.[32]

LEGAL ADVERTISING

In Virginia, legal advertising is a special area of the law that relates directly to newspapers. The law requires that certain actions by local governments be made public through local newspapers. Since the U.S. Supreme Court has ruled that the government cannot force such a publication upon newspapers,[33] local governments are required to buy advertising to publicize these legal actions.

Local governments often have a significant amount of legal advertising, some of which must be published weekly for four consecutive weeks.[34] The account for a county's legal advertising, therefore, can be quite lucrative.

Until 1992, legal advertisements could only be published in local newspapers that had histories of continuous publication, lists of paying subscribers, and second-class mailing permits.[35] An amendment to the law that year, however, made it possible for free-circulation newspapers to be designated as outlets for

---

[30] VA. CODE ANN. § 24.2-1001.5 (1950).
[31] Va. Code Ann. § 24.2-1007 (1950).
[32] Va. Code Ann. § 24.2-1003 (1950).
[33] Miami Herald v. Tornillo, 418 U.S. 241 (1974).
[34] VA. CODE ANN. § 8.01-323 (1950).
[35] VA. CODE ANN. § 8.01-324 (1950).

legal advertising. Free-circulation newspapers often have no second-class mailing permits because the bulk of their distribution is through newsstands, newsracks or unsolicited home delivery.

Under the law, a newspaper may petition a circuit court and may receive authority to publish legal advertising for up to a year if the newspaper has been published in the community for at least a year, employs a full-time news staff, reports local current events, has an editorial page, accepts letters to the editor, and has an audit of circulation certified by an independent auditing firm.[36] Over the years, the general assembly has made rumblings about the possibility of eliminating laws requiring legal advertising, but such efforts have yet to succeed.

Prior to the 1970s, advertising by lawyers was largely banned throughout the United States. In 1972, however, the U.S. Supreme Court held that such bans were unconstitutional.[37] In *Bates v. State Bar of Arizona,* the Court held that lawyer advertising was protected under the First Amendment as commercial speech. Since then, advertising by lawyers and law firms has become commonplace in the United States and Virginia.

The Virginia Bar has a clear set of guidelines for lawyer advertisements. These guidelines mirror much of the rules associated with commercial advertisements. Under the Virginia Rules of Professional Conduct, lawyers must be honest in their advertising of services and not make statements that are misleading to the public.[38] This includes a ban on

---

[36] *Id.*

[37] Bates v. State Bar of Ariz., 433 U.S. 350 (1977).

[38] VA. RULES OF PROF. CONDUCT RULE 7.1(a) (2013).

advertising specific case results without a required disclaimer.[39] All legal advertisements must contain the contact information of a person or firm who created the advertising content.[40] The rules also warn lawyers to be careful when advertising fees for services.[41] The Virginia Bar has created a hotline for lawyers to submit advertisements for review to ensure they are in compliance with the Rules of Professional Conduct.[42]

ADVERTISING AND THE COURTS

In the few advertising cases that have reached Virginia appellate courts, the courts have affirmed the government's right to regulate commercial speech,[43] but have not allowed blanket regulations.

In *Adams Outdoor Advertising v. Newport News,* for example, the Virginia Supreme Court struck down a city ordinance that regulated billboards.[44] The ordinance allowed on-site business signs that advertised services or products, but prohibited such signs off-site and also prohibited non-commercial on-site signs.[45] The court ruled that the ordinance discriminated against non-commercial advertising and held that it was unconstitutional.[46] Similarly, the Fourth U.S. Circuit Court of Appeals, in a Virginia case, found unconstitutional an Arlington County

---

[39] *Id. at* 7.1(b).

[40] *Id. at* 7.1 (c).

[41] *Id. at* 7.1, Comment 2.

[42] Checklist for Lawyers Who Advertise, http://www.vsb.org/site/regulation/checklist-for-lawyers-who-advertise (accessed Dec. 31, 2015).

[43] *See, e.g.,* Dotti v. Va. Bd. of Medicine, 407 S.E.2d 8 (Va. Ct. App. 1991).

[44] 373 S.E.2d 917 (Va. 1988).

[45] *Id.* at 918-21.

[46] *Id.* at 926-27.

ordinance limiting the number of signs that could be posted on private, residential property.[47]

In what may be the Virginia Supreme Court's most significant ruling involving advertising, the court held that a published newspaper advertisement was tantamount to a binding contract, even if the advertisement contained a typographical error. The case was *Chang v. First Colonial Savings Bank* and was based on a very narrow set of facts.[48] It began when Chia T. Chang and Shin S. Chang read a newspaper advertisement for a savings program offered by First Colonial Savings Bank. According to the advertisement, a depositor would receive a free color television set upon depositing $14,000 into a savings account that matured in three and one-half years. Upon maturity, according to the ad, the account would pay $20,136.12.

The Changs opened an account and received their television set, but three and one-half years later they were told that the ad contained a typographical error. It should have required a deposit of $15,000 rather than $14,000. They were also told that because they did not deposit $15,000, they would receive $18,823.93 instead of the higher figure.[49]

The Changs argued that the newspaper advertisement constituted an offer, which they accepted, establishing a contract under the law. The bank argued that the advertisement did not constitute an offer, but constituted an invitation to make an offer

---

[47] Arlington Cty. Republican Comm, v. Arlington Co., 983 F.2d 587 (4th Cir. 1993).

[48] 410 S.E.2d 928 (Va. 1991).

[49] *Id.* at 929.

to the general public, and that the Changs merely responded to the invitation.[50]

The court noted that newspaper advertisements are not generally considered offers under the law, "but merely invitations to bargain." The court noted a very narrow and limited exception to the rule, however: "Where the offer is clear, definite, and explicit, and leaves nothing open for negotiation, it constitutes an offer, acceptance of which will complete the contract."[51]

Therefore, the court held, the newspaper advertisement constituted an offer, which the Changs accepted. The fact that the ad contained a typographical error did not invalidate the contract because the bank did not inform the Changs of the mistake for three and one-half years and because "a unilateral mistake does not void an otherwise legally binding contract."[52]

Finally, it is important to note that at least one court has ruled that persons bringing actions based on allegations of false advertising may recover damages for personal injuries as well as for economic loss.[53]

---

[50] *Id.* at 929-30.

[51] *Id.* at 930.

[52] *Id.*

[53] Maldonado v. Nutri/System, Inc., 776 F. Supp. 278 (E.D. Va. 1991).

11. PORNOGRAPHY & OBSCENITY

Few debates over free expression issues possess more passion than those related to pornography and obscenity.[1] The distribution of sexually explicit material has been the subject of two federal commissions and countless studies, experiments and lawsuits.[2]

Unfortunately, the debate over how material related to sex should be regulated or distributed in society often borders on the absurd. The works of William Shakespeare, James Joyce, John Steinbeck and William Faulkner have been attacked – along with genuine smut – as pornographic. A debate over the types of books that children could check out of the public library in one eastern North Carolina county

---

[1] The terms "pornography" and "obscenity" are not synonymous. Pornography generally deals with material related to sex, as does erotica. While some dictionaries treat pornography and erotica as synonyms, in modern usage, erotica is generally considered to be sexual, without being degrading, while pornography is generally considered to be material that treats people – usually women – as sexual objects. Both erotica and pornography, except for child pornography, are legal in the United States. Obscene pornography, on the other hand, may be banned and distributors and producers may be punished. Pornography becomes obscene when it meets specific criteria. *See* John Watson, *Regulating Pornography, in* COMMUNICATION AND THE LAW 69 (W. Wat Hopkins ed. 2016 ed.); and discussion accompanying *infra* notes 4-5. Child pornography, that is, sexually explicit material involving persons under the age of 18, is illegal. *See* New York v. Ferber, 458 U.S. 747 (1982).

[2] *See, generally,* W. WAT HOPKINS, MR. JUSTICE BRENNAN AND FREEDOM OF EXPRESSION 19-49 (1991); Watson, *supra* note 1, at 75-78.

three decades ago prompted the librarian to classify the Bible as "adult non-fiction" and require parental consent before a minor could peruse that book.

In Virginia, the absurdity has extended to Carroll County, where, in 1992, a small group of parents pushed school officials to force an English teacher to stop using an award-winning book in class, then tried to have the teacher fired. The book contained language to which the parents objected. And, in 1997, prosecutors in Roanoke, because of a few vocal objections, prosecuted a nightclub operator for allowing nude dancing in a club that was closed to all persons except adults. This, despite the fact that much more objectionable material was available in video stores, which remain untouched by law enforcement. The same year, a judge in Prince William County gave his stamp of approval to what was tantamount to a Star Chamber proceeding. Judge Dixon Foster allowed a prosecutor to keep secret the names of members of a committee who – by deciding whether videotapes and other materials violate community standards – helped select persons to be prosecuted on obscenity charges.[3]

These examples – few among many – demonstrate that when sexual material is involved, reason often is not.

IS IT OBSCENE?

The face of obscenity law has changed often in the United States, but since the U.S. Supreme Court's

---

[3] *County "Obscenity Panel" Members Can Remain Anonymous,* 3 NEWS MEDIA UPDATE 13, Aug. 25, 1997, http://www.rcfp.org.

1973 ruling in *Miller v. California,*[4] the test for determining whether pornographic material is obscene has not changed. In that case, the Court held that material is obscene if it meets three criteria:

> (a) whether "the average person, applying contemporary community standards" would find that the work, taken as a whole, appeals to the prurient interest; . . . (b) whether the work depicts or describes in a patently offensive way, sexual conduct specifically defined by the applicable state law; and (c) whether the work, taken as a whole, lacks serious literary, artistic, political, or scientific value.[5]

A person may be punished for producing or distributing sexually explicit material only if that material is determined by a jury to be obscene, and to be obscene it must meet all three points of the Miller Test. The first point of the Miller Test invokes a local test, the second invokes a state test, and the third invokes a national test. A local jury, however, ultimately examines the material in light of all three points to determine whether it is obscene so, to some extent, all prosecutions for obscenity invoke local "contemporary community standards."

Contemporary Community Standards

In the years following the Supreme Court's first obscenity case, *Roth v. United States*[6] in 1957, there

---

[4] 413 U.S. 15 (1973).

[5] *Id.* at 24.

[6] 354 U.S. 476 (1957).

was some controversy among members of the Court as to whether local or national standards should apply when jurors determine whether sexually explicit material is obscene.[7] Chief Justice Warren Burger, who wrote the majority opinion in *Miller,* cleared up that controversy – though he may have initiated another. Chief Justice Burger made it very clear that the contemporary community standards of a local community must be considered in determining whether material is obscene. He wrote: "It is neither realistic nor constitutionally sound to read the First Amendment as requiring that the people of Maine or Mississippi accept public depiction of conduct found tolerable in Las Vegas or New York City."[8]

More than forty years after *Miller,* however, courts in Virginia still have little guidance as to what "contemporary community standards" are and how they are to be applied. Two 1997 obscenity trials demonstrate the complexity and lack of understanding of the issue.

In October 1997, the owner of the nightclub Girls, Girls, Girls, Inc., was indicted on fifteen counts of violating the state's obscenity law and on fifteen counts of violating Roanoke's anti-nudity law. The attorney for the club attempted to introduce evidence demonstrating that the local community standards allowed for nude entertainment, but the judge in the case refused to allow the evidence. Jack Kennett wanted to show a portion of a video of the movie *Oh!*

---

[7] *See, e.g.,* Jacobellis v. Ohio, 378 U.S. 184, 193-95 (1964)(opinion of Brennan, J., joined by Goldberg, J.,); *id.* at 200 (Warren, C.J., dissenting).

[8] 413 U.S. at 32.

Calcutta, because a live production of the show had been performed at the Roanoke Civic Center. He also wanted to show portions of sexually explicit movies that were available for rent in local video stores. The trial judge, however, refused to admit the evidence.[9]

In addition, Assistant Commonwealth's Attorney Dennis Nagel introduced no evidence whatsoever on the question of contemporary community standards. The prosecutor simply showed jurors grainy videotapes of the nude performances at Girls, Girls, Girls, Inc.

The jury convicted the club's owner of fourteen counts of violating the anti-nudity statute, but only one count of violating the obscenity statute. Fines totaled $40,000.[10]

The clear indication is that, in Roanoke at least, jurors automatically know what contemporary community standards are.

The same is not true in Wythe County, however. Seven weeks after the Roanoke convictions, Wythe County General District Judge Daniel Bird ruled that community standards must be specified before there can be convictions for violating those standards. In the absence of evidence determining contemporary community standards, Bird ruled, six

---

[9] *See* Lawrence Hammack, *Yes, Nude Dancing Art, Says Scholar,* ROANOKE TIMES, Oct. 1, 1997, at A1.

[10] *See* Lawrence Hammack, *Jury Finds No Art in "Girls" Act; Club Fined $40,000 Maximum,* ROANOKE TIMES, Oct. 2, 1997, at A1.

people connected with a strip show could not be convicted on obscenity-related charges.[11]

Applicable State Law

The second point of the Miller Test places a unique burden upon states. It requires them to define, specifically, the types of sexual conduct that may not be depicted or described "in a patently offensive way." Without that state definition, there can be no conviction for creating or distributing obscene pornography.

By the time the Supreme Court had delivered its opinion in *Miller,* many states, including Virginia, had defined obscenity. In 1971, the Virginia General Assembly defined it this way:

> [T]hat which considered as a whole has as its dominant theme or purpose an appeal to prurient interest, that is, a shameful or morbid interest in nudity, sex, or excretion, and if it goes substantially beyond customary limits of candor in description or representation of such matters.[12]

The definition drew on language that appeared in *Roth v. United States.* In *Roth,* the Court, for the first time, held that obscene material lay outside the protection of the First Amendment, and the Court defined very generally terms the term "obscenity." The

---

[11] *See* Paul Dellinger, *Judge: To Convict, Wythe Must Define Standards of Obscenity,* ROANOKE TIMES, Nov. 25, 1997, at A1.

[12] VA. CODE § 18.1-227 (1950).

Court adjusted the definition of obscenity between 1957 and 1973,[13] but in *Miller,* a majority of the Court, for the first time since *Roth,* agreed upon a new definition for the term.

Virginia's broad definition of obscenity did not change, however, and, after 1973, the state statute did not appear to follow the mandate of *Miller* that definitions of obscenity be specific.

In fact, that very issue was addressed in a case called *Price v. Commonwealth.*[14] Bobby J. Price was sentenced to twelve months in prison and ordered to pay a $1,000 fine for showing the movie *Anomalies* in his Danville theater.[15] He appealed the conviction, arguing that Virginia's definition of obscenity was vague and overbroad under the *Miller* ruling.[16] The Virginia Supreme Court disagreed, holding that the statute was constitutional.[17]

The court based the ruling on its previous interpretations of the obscenity statute. Five years earlier, the court had reversed the conviction of a bookstore operator for selling copies of the magazines

---

13 *See, e.g.,* A Book Named "John Cleland's Memoirs of a Woman of Pleasure" v. Massachusetts, 383 U.S. 413 (1966).

14 The *Price* case demonstrates the complicated nature of the obscenity issue. The case reached the state supreme court twice before all the issues could be settled. *Price v. Commonwealth,* 189 S.E.2d 324 (Va. 1972), is generally called *Price I,* and *Price v. Commonwealth*, 201 S.E.2d 798 (Va. 1974) is generally called *Price II.*

15 *Price I,* 189 S.E.2d at 316.

16 *Price II,* 201 S.E.2d at 799.

17 *Id.* at 800-01.

Knight and *Raw.*[18] These girlie magazines only depicted nudity, the court said, and, therefore, were not obscene.[19]

That interpretation considerably narrowed the broad nature of the obscenity statue, the Virginia Supreme Court held in *Price II.* Under the statute, therefore, only "hard core pornography" is prohibited. And, as interpreted by the court, the statue limits "hard core pornography" to "portrayals of sexual activity or excretion, not including mere nudity, which go beyond the customary limits of candor in representing such matters."[20] The statute, therefore, the court held, adheres to the requirements of *Miller* and is constitutional.

In 1975, the Virginia General Assembly altered the definition of obscenity slightly, so that it now proscribes material

> [W]hich, considered as a whole, has as its dominant theme or purpose an appeal to the prurient interest in sex, that is, a shameful or morbid interest in nudity, sexual conduct, sexual excitement, excretory functions or products thereof or sadomasochistic abuse, and which goes substantially beyond customary limits of candor in description or representation of such matters and which, taken as a whole,

---

[18] House v. Commonwealth, 169 S.E.2d 572, 573 (Va. 1969).

[19] *Id.* at 577.

[20] *Price II,* 201 S.E.2d at 800.

does not have serious literary, artistic, political or scientific value.[21]

Serious Value

Sexually explicit material is not obscene if it contains serious value. Under *Miller*, of course, that value may be literary, artistic, political or scientific. *Miller* also requires that the work be taken as a whole when the determination of value is made. And the U.S. Supreme Court has held that the determination of value be made based on national, rather than state or local, standards.[22]

Like the first point of the Miller Test, the procedure for determining value in Virginia has a spotted history. No obscenity case turning on the issue of value has reached the Virginia Supreme Court.

Who May Sue

Virginia law prohibits obscene material in a wide variety of forms: books, pamphlets, photographs, magazines, films, videos, bumper stickers, objects or recordings.[23] It is also unlawful to exhibit any obscene object or performance,[24] to advertise any obscene performances[25] or to photograph or allow the photography of any person, including oneself, for use in obscene material.[26] In addition, any town, city or

---

[21] VA. CODE § 18.2-372 (1950).

[22] Pope v. Illinois, 481 U.S. 497 (1987).

[23] VA. CODE § 18.2-373 (1950).

[24] VA. CODE § 18.2-375 (1950).

[25] VA. CODE § 18.2-376 (1950).

[26] VA. CODE § 18.2-382 (1950).

county can adopt additional ordinances against obscenity.[27]

The law places no restrictions on who may bring an action to determine whether material is obscene. Anyone, the law says, may petition the court to determine whether a book is obscene.[28] When such a petition is filed, a judge will examine the book to determine whether there is probable cause, and will either order a hearing to determine the obscenity of the work, or will dismiss the action. If a hearing is to be held, the judge may order that the book not be sold until after the hearing.

During the hearing, evidence may be introduced concerning the value of the book, the reaction of the public to the work, the intent and reputation of the author and publisher, the method of promoting the book and the prurient appeal of the book.

The judge must issue a written determination of his finding, which may be appealed.

REGULATING PORNOGRAPHY

Obscene material, as previously indicated, may be banned, and its producers and distributors may be punished. Material may focus on sexual matters,

---

[27] VA. CODE § 18.2-389 (1950).

[28] VA. CODE § 18.2-384 (1950). The Virginia statute discussed here refers only to judicial proceedings related to books. The federal appellate courts in Virginia, however, have held that films should be accorded the same protection as books, and the same type proceeding should be applied to film. *See* Tyrone v. Wilkinson, 410 F.2d 639 (4th Cir. 1969); Greenmount Sales, Inc. v. Davila, 344 F. Supp. 860, 864 (E.D. Va. 1972), *aff'd in part and rev'd in part* 479 F.2d 591 (4th Cir. 1973).

however, and not be obscene. The U.S. Supreme Court has noted that sexuality and obscenity are not synonymous.[29]

The production and distribution of pornography may be allowed by the First Amendment, but regulation of pornography is also allowed. Both the U.S. Supreme Court and the Virginia Supreme Court, for example, have held that child pornography is illegal.[30] Virginia state law prohibits both the production and possession of child pornography.[31] In addition, state law prohibits the use of communication systems such as computer networks and bulletin boards to promote child pornography.[32]

The commonwealth also prohibits the sale of sexually explicit material to minors.[33] Indeed, the commonwealth attempts to keep minors from even seeing such material on display in newsstands or bookstores. A state law requires that sexually explicit material that may be harmful to minors must be displayed in a way so that minors cannot examine that material.[34] Following a legal dispute that lasted some five years, the statute has been held to be constitutional.[35]

---

[29] Roth v. United States, 354 U.S. 476, 487 (1957).

[30] New York v. Ferber, 458 U.S. 747 (1982); Freeman v. Commonwealth, 288 S.E.2d 461 (1982).

[31] VA. CODE § 18.2-374.1 & § 18.2-374.1:1 (1950).

[32] VA. CODE § 18.2-374.3 (1950).

[33] VA. CODE § 18.2-391(a) (1950).

[34] *Id.*

[35] American Booksellers Ass'n, Inc. v. Commonwealth, 882 F.2d 125 (4th Cir. 1989), *cert. denied,* 494 U.S. 1056 (1990).

The commonwealth has also attempted to restrict sexually explicit material from prisoners. A federal court upheld a policy of the Keene Mountain Correctional Center in Oakwood in denying two prisoners copies of *Gallery* magazine.[36] The court found that sexually explicit publications have a negative impact on the security, discipline, order, public safety and rehabilitation of prisoners.[37] The Fourth U.S. Circuit Court of Appeals, however, reversed the district court's ruling, holding that the publishers of the magazines in question had a First Amendment right to present a challenge to the policy.[38] The ruling did not impact the holding that the material may be restricted – only that publishers must be given notice so they may challenge the restrictions.

A statute that has not been tested in court prohibits theater operators from showing previews for movies that carry motion picture ratings more restrictive than the movies being shown.[39] Under the statute, for example, a preview for an R-rated movie could not accompany the showing of a PG-13 movie.

In addition, the Virginia Supreme Court has upheld the regulation of nudity in bars and other establishments. As the experiences in Roanoke and Wythe County demonstrate, when dancers go from

---

[36] Hodges v. Commonwealth, 871 F. Supp. 873 (W.D. Va. 1994), *rev'd* 80 F.3d 105 (4th Cir. 1996), *cert. denied by* Angelone v. Montcalm Publ'g Corp. v. Beck, 519 U.S. 928 (1996).

[37] *Id.* at 877.

[38] Montcalm Publ'g Corp. v. Beck, 80 F.3d 105 (4th Cir. 1996), *cert. denied* 519 U.S. 928 (1996).

[39] VA. CODE § 18.2-386 (1950).

being topless to being completely nude, they are tempting prosecutors and are likely to face obscenity charges.[40]

Finally, jurisdictions are capitalizing on a ruling by the Virginia Supreme Court allowing topless bars to be regulated. In *Wayside Restaurant, Inc. v. Virginia Beach,* the court upheld a Virginia Beach ordinance prohibiting public nudity as applied to bars.[41] The ordinance prohibited the exposing of "male or female genitals, pubic area or buttocks with less than a fully opaque covering, or the showing of the female breast with less than a fully opaque covering of any portion thereof below the top of the nipple."[42]

In the wake of the case, a number of jurisdictions have approved ordinances prohibiting public nudity. The ordinances are aimed specifically at prohibiting topless dancing.[43] Such ordinances have been upheld a constitutional by the U.S. Supreme Court.[44]

---

[40] *See supra* notes 9-11 and accompanying discussion.

[41] 208 S.E.2d 51 (Va. 1974).

[42] *Id.* at 52 n.1.

[43] *See, e.g.,* Kathy Loan, *Strip Club Is Back,* ROANOKE TIMES, Jan. 25, 1996, at C1.

[44] *See* Erie v. Pap's A.M., 529 U.S. 277 (2000).

12. STUDENT EXPRESSION IN VIRGINIA

Student expression has always held a tenuous position under the law. As persons, students are entitled to the protections granted by the Constitution. Many students are not adults, however, so they do not enjoy full access to constitutional rights and privileges. They may not vote, for example, buy alcoholic beverages or drive cars until they reach legally specified ages.

Similarly, in many circumstances, they are not allowed to express themselves with the full vigor adults enjoy. The U.S. Supreme Court has recognized that young people enjoy the right of free expression and, to paraphrase the Court, that they do not shed that right at the schoolhouse gate.[1] But other factors govern the degree and extent of student speech. While young people are at school, for example, the elementary and high school administrators and teachers under whose care those young people fall, operate *in loco parentis* – in the place of parents. The law recognizes that these school officials can exercise some control over students – including the way students express themselves – in order to ensure that the function of the school setting is maintained and the students are insulated from inappropriate material.

While recognizing the free speech rights of students, therefore, the Court has also allowed school

---

[1] Tinker v. Des Moines Indep. Sch. Dist., 393 U.S. 503, 506 (1969).

officials to restrict and punish offensive speech.[2] The Court has also held that a principal has the authority to unilaterally censor a high school newspaper if the principal does not believe material in the newspaper fits into the pedagogical goals of the school.[3] But, while expressive conduct on school grounds may be restricted,[4] courts have been reluctant to prohibit the distribution of literature unless there is a likelihood the distribution will cause disruption.[5]

In general, speech issues involving students fall into two categories: freedom of the student press and free speech rights on school property.

Freedom of the High School Press

In the 1988 case *Hazelwood School District v. Kuhlmeier,* the U.S. Supreme Court ruled that a principal could censor a high school newspaper because he believed the material published in the newspaper to be inappropriate for students in his school. The principal pulled two pages from the school paper without consulting either student editors or the newspaper's advisor.[6]

Until that ruling, the high school press enjoyed

---

[2] *See, e.g.,* Bethel Sch. Dist. v. Fraser, 478 U.S. 675 (1986).

[3] Hazelwood Sch. Dist. v. Kuhlmeier, 484 U.S. 260 (1988).

[4] *See* Crosby v. Holsinger, 852 F.2d 801 (4th Cir. 1988).

[5] *See* Baughman v. Freienmuth, 478 F.2d 1345 (4th Cir. 1973); Quarterman v. Byrd, 453 F.2d 54 (4th Cir. 1971). *Baughman* is a Maryland case, and *Quarterman is* a North Carolina case, but both opinions are from the Fourth Circuit, which also holds jurisdiction over Virginia. *See also* Williams v. Spencer, 622 F.2d 1200 (4th Cir. 1980); Leibner v. Sharbaugh, 429 F. Supp. 744 (E.D.Va. 1977).

[6] 484 U.S. at 261.

significant freedom. Many courts, including the Fourth U.S. Circuit Court of Appeals, which holds jurisdiction over Virginia, ruled that high school newspapers were public forums and could not be regulated by school administrators on the basis of content.[7]

Much has changed, however.

Since *Hazelwood,* the Student Press Law Center of Washington, D.C., which is dedicated to freedom of the student press, has reported an increase in the number of calls from student editors facing administrative censorship.[8] In addition, anecdotal evidence from across Virginia indicates that school administrators are taking a more aggressive role in controlling the student press.[9]

The Student Press Law Center recommends that high school editors combat potential censorship in two ways. First, the center recommends that editors encourage state legislators to pass legislation protecting the high school press from unwarranted censorship. The center has developed model legislation that can be sent to legislators which, if passed, would protect school-sponsored publications, even if those publications are published in conjunction with classes.

The legislation allows regulation of obscenity, defamation, invasion of privacy and material that

---

[7] *See* Gambino v. Fairfax Co. School Bd., 564 F.2d 157 (4th Cir. 1977), *aff'g* 429 F. Supp. 731 (E.D.Va. 1977).

[8] The address of the Student Press Law Center is 1608 Rhode Island Avenue, NW, Suite 211, Washington, D.C., 20036; the phone number is (202) 785-5450; the Web site is http://www.splc.org.

[9] *See, e.g., Advisor Submits to Prior Review Policy*, SPLC REPORT, Winter 1989-90, at 25

would cause a substantial disruption at school, but gives student editors protection in determining the news, opinion and advertising content of their publications and prohibits prior review of student publications by administrators.

The Student Press Law Center also recommends that student publications specifically identify themselves as public forums for student expression. The center reports that the Supreme Court indicated that "if the Hazelwood School District had been operating under a policy that described its student publications as forums for student expression, it would not have allowed non-disruptive stories about teen pregnancy and divorce to be censored."[10]

Copies of the model legislation and model guidelines for identification as a public forum are available from the Student Press Law Center and are published in *Law of the Student Press,* a handbook published by the center.[11]

Freedom of high school press in Virginia has reached the court in an unusual case from Loudoun County. In 2004, Edward Myers, the parent of three children in Loudoun County's public schools, wanted to run an advertisement in the Sugarland Elementary Yearbook criticizing the use of the Pledge of Allegiance. Myers was a Anabaptist Mennonite who claimed his religion mandated a separation of church and state in education. In his proposed advertisement, he wanted the following printed: "Tired of civil

---

[10] STUDENT PRESS LAW CENTER, LAW OF THE STUDENT PRESS 96 (1985).

[11] The Student Press Law Center model legislation is found in LAW OF THE STUDENT PRESS, *id.* at 94; guidelines for designing a student newspaper as a public forum are found *id.* at 97.

religion exercises in public schools? Try this pledge alternative: I pledge hell's legions to the rag of the united states of hysteria, and screw the public, make them stand, one nation, dumber than cod, so liberty and justice fall."[12]

The advertisement request was denied by the school's principle citing the fact that the request was untimely.[13] Later Myers submitted another advertisement for the athletic program which included the Web site http://www.CivilReligionSucks.com as well as "flag desecration products."[14] Again his request was denied because of the language used in the advertisement. Myers sued the school district citing that the school's refusal to allow him to run these advertisements in school publications violated his First Amendment rights.[15] The federal court for the Eastern District of Virginia disagreed, finding that under *Hazelwood* that Myers's advertisements in school newspapers could be editorially controlled because they are part of the school's curriculum. As for Myers's athletic program advertisement, the court held that the school could legally reject it for publication as well. Because the word "sucks" appeared in the advertisement the court held that under Hazelwood the

---

[12] Myers v. Loudon Cty. Sch. Bd., 500 F. Supp. 2d 539, 542 (E.D. Va. 2007).

[13] *Id.*

[14] *Id.*

[15] Myers attempted several activities protesting what he viewed as school-endorsed religion, including passing out pamphlets on sidewalks in front of the school, asking the school to distribute flyers in homeroom classes outlining his protests about school policies, and submitting an advertisement to the county's high school newspaper. Among the issues analyzed by the court were an Establishment Clause issue as well as right to petition the government. *Myers*, 500 F. Supp. 2d at 545-47.

school could ban disruptive speech that is made on school property.[16]

Freedom of the University Press

The Supreme Court's ruling in *Hazelwood* does not affect the student press at public universities, at least not in Virginia and other states within the Fourth U.S. Circuit Court of Appeals. That court ruled in a North Carolina case that the student press at public universities operates as a public forum and may not be regulated by university officials, even if mandatory student fees pay for the production of the newspaper.[17]

While *Hazelwood* overruled similar rulings related to the high school press, cases related to universities remain intact. Student newspapers that are not part of a university's curriculum, therefore, may not be censored and may not be subjected to prior review by administrators.[18]

---

[16] The U.S. District Court for the Eastern District of Virginia ruled that the rejection of the yearbook advertisement was not content based because it was a matter of timeliness of the submission. Because there was no evidence to the contrary the court found that no constitutional issues were triggered by its rejection. Myers, 500 F. Supp. 2d at 554.

[17] Joyner v. Whiting, 477 F.2d 456 (4th Cir. 1973). The role of "legislative motive" of the government in regulating public forums has been questioned by the Fourth Circuit in *Sons of Confederate Veterans v. City of Lexington*, 722 F.3d 224, 232 (4th Cir. 2013). In that case, the Fourth Circuit held that the government can limit any speech in a designated public forum. The government's underlying reasons for passing laws regulating public forums is irrelevant in the analysis. A deeper analysis of this issue can be found in Chapter 3.

[18] It is important to note that the U.S. Court of Appeals for the Seventh Circuit, which does not cover Virginia, disagrees. In a 2005 case, the court held in an en banc decision that college administrators could review material in a college newspaper. In

In addition, the U.S. Supreme Court, in 1994, affirmed the proposition that student publications at public universities could not be denied funding on the basis of content – even if the content is religious. *Rosenberger v. Rector and Visitors of the University of Virginia*[19] is an important case for advocates of free speech for students.

The case began when Wide Awake Productions, a student organization at the University of Virginia, sought funding for its publication, *Wide Awake: A Christian Perspective at the University of Virginia.* The funding was denied on grounds that the publication promoted a Christian viewpoint. Attorneys for the university argued that the university had limited funding and was required to establish some mechanism for distributing those limited funds. One method, the university argued, was denying funds to organizations that used publications to promote religious viewpoints.[20] The Supreme Court, however, ruled that the university could not use viewpoint discrimination as a basis for distributing funds.[21] To do so, the Court held, violates the First Amendment.[22]

Newspapers at private colleges and universities, however, enjoy significantly less freedom. Private colleges and universities are not considered to be part of the government; they operate on private rather than

---

that case, Judge Frank Easterbrook wrote that the *Hazelwood* framework was applicable to college newspapers. However, this approach to college newspapers is in the minority of circuits. *See* Hosty v. Carter, 412 F.3d 731 (7th Cir. 2005) (en banc), *cert. denied,* 546 U.S. 1169 (2006).

[19] 515 U.S. 819 (1995).

[20] *Id.* at 832-33.

[21] *Id.* at 835.

[22] *Id.* at 837.

public funds. The First Amendment of the Constitution restricts the state from abridging the freedom of the press, but not private institutions, so private colleges and universities can presume to be publishers of student newspapers. Administrators, therefore, have authority to replace editors, fire advisors and control the content of the student press. While this may be pedagogically unsound, it is legal.[23]

Student editors at public institutions might have significant freedom from regulations imposed by their colleges or universities, but because of their independence they are increasingly the targets of lawsuits. Indeed, the *Collegiate Times*, the student newspaper at Virginia Tech, faced two lawsuits in 1997, both of which were resolved in 1998.

Sharon Yeagle, a mid-level administrator at Tech, sued the newspaper when editors forgot to change a line in a template used to design the newspaper and, as a result, she was identified as "Director of Butt Licking."[24] The line appeared under Yeagle's name in a graphic display of a quotation accompanying a news story. When the template was used to set off the quote, editors failed to replace the line with Yeagle's actual title, assistant to the vice president of student affairs. Editors attempted to apologize to Yeagle, who refused to talk to them and, instead, sued for defamation. The Virginia Supreme Court upheld a circuit court ruling dismissing the case because, in the words of the supreme court, "[T]he

---

[23] For a discussion of the pedagogical ramifications of student press restrictions, *see* W. Wat Hopkins, *Hazelwood v. Kuhlmeier: Sound Constitutional Law, Unsound Pedagogy,* 16 N. KY. L. REV. 521 (1989).

[24] Yeagle v. Collegiate Times, 497 S.E.2d 136, 137 (Va. 1998).

phrase at issue could not reasonably be considered as conveying factual information."[25]

The second suit against the *Collegiate Times* was filed by Tony Morrison, a former football player at Tech who was charged with but never indicted for rape. Morrison sued the paper for an editorial critical of the administration's handling of the case. He claimed that the editorial falsely charged him with committing a crime.[26] In May 1998, the suit was dismissed on a motion by Morrison's attorney.[27]

While both suits border on the ludicrous, they demonstrate that student journalists are not immune from legal action simply because they are students.

FREEDOM OF STUDENT EXPRESSION

The courts allow school administrators significant leeway in controlling access to school property for the purpose of expressive conduct and control of what may be called school-sponsored speech.

Federal courts in Virginia, for example, have ruled that school officials had the right to ban the "Johnny Reb" symbol as a school mascot because the

---

[25] *Id.* at 139. It is important to note that determining whether statements made could potentially be viewed as true is fact sensitive. The Circuit Court of Chesterfield County ruled that criticisms made against a faculty member by her colleagues could potentially be viewed as true. In that case the plaintiff alleged colleagues had called her "mean," "uncooperative," and a "troublemaking Republican." Cobbs v. Commonwealth, 55 Va. Cir. 1, 3, 5 (Cir. Court 2001) (Chesterfield County).

[26] Morrison v. Padalino, 760 CL 96 B02902-00 (Richmond Cir., filed Nov. 27, 1996).

[27] Ian Zack, *Ex-Player's Newspaper Suit Dismissed,* ROANOKE TIMES, May 6, 1998, at B4.

symbol was offensive to blacks at the school[28] and suspend a student for wearing a shirt saying "Drugs Suck!"[29] This issue of student expression on clothing became an issue again in 2015 when 17 Christiansburg High School students were suspended for wearing Confederate flag emblems on their clothes. The suspension came one month after the school told students to remove Confederate flag bumper stickers from their vehicles. [30]

Virginia courts have also ruled that high school principals may ban from campus students who participated in disruptive conduct – such as sit-ins or protests. And those students who do not leave campuses when ordered to do so may be charged with trespassing.[31] The same is true for colleges and universities.[32] University restrictions on expressive

---

[28] Crosby v. Holsinger, 852 F.2d 801 (4th Cir. 1988).

[29] Broussard v. Sch. Bd. of Norfolk, 801 F. Supp. 1526 (E.D. Va. 1992).

[30] *See, e.g.,* Justin Ward, *17 Christiansburg High School Students Suspended After Wearing Confederate Flags on Clothing*, WDBJ-7, Sept. 17, 2015, http://www.wdbj7.com/news/local/more-than-20-christiansburg-high-student-out-of-class-after-weating-confederate-flags-on-clothing/35321294; T. Rees Shapiro & Moriah Balingit, *Virginia High School Students Suspended for Wearing Confederate Flag Apparel*, WASH. POST, Sept. 17, 2015, *available at* https://www.washingtonpost.com/news/education/wp/2015/09/17/virginia-high-school-students-suspended-for-wearing-confederate-flag-apparel/.

[31] Pleasants v. Commonwealth, 203 S.E.2d 114 (Va. 1974).

[32] Johnson v. Commonwealth, 186 S.E.2d 53 (Va. 1972), *cert. denied*, 407 U.S. 925 (1972).

conduct, however, must be content neutral[33] and must allow demonstrations at some locations on campus.[34]

In 2009, the U.S. Supreme Court, in *Morse v. Frederick,* held that restrictions on high school student expression even extended beyond the classroom.[35] That case involved Joseph Frederick, a Juneau, Alaska, high school student, who was suspended from his high school for holding up a 14-foot banner that said "Bong Hits 4 Jesus" while an Olympic Torch relay passed by his high school.[36] The high school allowed students to watch the relay from the sidewalk in front of the school as a school sanctioned field trip. Frederick was suspended under a school board policy that prohibited the endorsement of minors using illegal substances. Frederick appealed his suspension citing that the school board's policy violated his First Amendment rights. The U.S. Supreme Court disagreed. Writing for the majority Chief Justice John Roberts held that schools and school boards are allowed to regulate their students as they see fit. This may include the limitation of student speech. The Court held that in *Bethel School District v. Fraser* it was clear that First Amendment rights of students were "not automatically coextensive with the rights of adults,"[37] and that the "mode of analysis set forth in *Tinker* is not absolute."[38]

---

[33] Sword v. Fox, 446 F.2d 1091 (4th Cir. 1971), *cert. denied,* 404 U.S. 994 (1971).

[34] Students Against Apartheid Coalition v. O'Neil, 838 F.2d 735 (4th. Cir. 1988).

[35] 551 U.S. 393 (2007).

[36] *Id.* at 407 (citing Verona School District 47J v. Action, 515 U.S. 646, 661 (1995)).

[37] *Id.* at 404 (citing Bethel School District v. Fraser, 478 U.S. 675, 682 (1986)).

[38] *Id.* at 405.

Chief Justice Roberts held that the school board's policy of banning student speech that promotes illegal drug use was "an 'important—indeed, perhaps compelling' interest."[39]

Colleges and universities also have authority to control access to campuses, even when the purpose of access is simply to express opinions. Virginia Tech refused to grant an itinerant preacher permission to preach on the university's Drill Field because the preacher, James G. Gilles, was not sponsored by an individual or group affiliated with the university. Circumventing university policy, officials gave Gilles permission to preach at the school's outdoor amphitheater, a secluded spot that received little traffic. Gilles sued, but the Fourth Circuit refused to rule on the merits of the case. The court held that Gilles could not show that he had been prevented from preaching because he could not gain sponsorship.[40]

The court recognized that it was dancing around the issue, but blamed the parties for prompting an opinion that was technical rather than substantive:

> We do not foreclose the possibility that some justiciable case will arise between these parties in the future. At that time, however, the record

---

[39] *Id.* at 407. In his concurring opinion in *Morse v. Frederick*, Justice Clarence Thomas was extremely critical of the *Tinker* decision because it was not in line with what he viewed as the history of teachers acting *in loco parentis*. Justice Thomas wrote, "[B]ecause *Tinker* utterly ignored the history of public education, courts (including this one) routinely find it necessary to create *ad hoc* exceptions to its central premise. This doctrine of exceptions creates confusion without fixing the underlying problem by returning to first principles." 551 U.S. at 421 (Thomas, J., concurring).

[40] Gilles v. Torgersen, 71 F.3d 497, 499 (4th Cir. 1995).

> may reveal what it does not reveal now – namely, the reasons for denying Gilles access to the precise forum he sought and his precise challenge to those reasons. As it is, the parties are jousting over a sponsorship requirement that is not being invoked to bar Gilles from speaking on campus, and they are ignoring whatever time, place or manner guideline is presumably being used to prohibit him from speaking on the drillfield. In other words, the true controversy is eluding the court, while a false one is proposed.[41]

Despite the court's disclaimer, Gilles was denied the right to preach on the Drill Field simply because officials at a major university said he couldn't.

Had Gilles chosen to distribute handbills on or around the Drill Field announcing that he would later be preaching at the amphitheater, however, he would likely have been able to do so. Not even high school principals have the right to ban the distribution of literature at their schools, unless regulations are narrowly drawn and specific as to the types of literature that may not be distributed.[42]

In addition, as demonstrated in *Rosenberger,* courts have been hesitant to limit student expression on the basis of content, even when the expression is obnoxious. When the Sigma Chi Fraternity at George Mason University held an womanless beauty contest, for example, in which members of the fraternity portrayed stereotypical images of different types of women, the university responded by suspending the

---

[41] *Id.* at 501.

[42] *See* cases cited at *supra* note 5.

fraternity and placing it on a two-year probation.[43] The Fourth Circuit called the performance "an exercise of teenage campus excess,"[44] but held, nevertheless, that it was still inherently expressive and, thus, entitled to First Amendment protection.[45]

---

[43] *See* Iota Xi Chapter of Sigma Chi Fraternity v. George Mason Univ., 993 F.2d 386, 388 (4th Cir. 1993).

[44] *Id.* at 389.

[45] *Id.* at 390.

CASE INDEX

D

E

F

G

H

I

J

K

P

Q

R

S

T

U

V

W

Y

SUBJECT INDEX

A

B

C

G

H

I

J

K

L

M

N

O

P

U

V

W

Y

ABOUT THE AUTHORS

W. Wat Hopkins is a professor of communication at Virginia Tech, where he teaches journalism and communication law. He has a master's degree in journalism and a Ph.D. degree in mass communication research, both from the University of North Carolina at Chapel Hill. He was a reporter for seven years in South Carolina and North Carolina before he began teaching. He taught journalism in North Carolina and Arkansas before moving to Virginia. He has written widely and has made a number of presentations on First Amendment topics. Mass Communication Law in Virginia is his third book. He is also editor and an author of a major national textbook on communication law. He and his wife, Roselynn, have three sons, one grandson and two granddaughters.

Cayce Myers is an assistant professor in the Department of Communication at Virginia Tech where he teaches public relations. Prior to entering academia he worked as an attorney in Georgia handling a variety of civil and criminal matters in federal and state courts. He has a Ph.D. in mass communication from the University of Georgia, Henry W. Grady College of Journalism and Mass Communication, an LL.M. from the University of Georgia School of Law, and a J.D. from Mercer University Walter F. George School of Law. His research focuses on laws affecting public relations practice, specifically regulations on social media, commercial speech, and the Internet. He is the legal research editor for the Institute for Public Relations.

Made in the USA
Columbia, SC
08 January 2020

86265718R00163